Neil a Random Man

Neil a Random Man

By:
Anoop Taneja

ADROIT

Adroit Publishers
NEW DELHI • KATHMANDU

Published by ADROIT PUBLISHERS
4675/21, Ganpati Bhawan, Ansari Road,
Daryaganj, New Delhi-110 002, INDIA, Phone : 011-4558 3612
Mob: 8750888466, E-mail: adroitpublishers@gmail.com

This is a work of fiction. Names, characters, places and Incidents are either the product of the author's imagination or are used fictitiously, and any resemblance to any actual persons, living or dead, events or locales is entirely coincidental.

ISBN : 978-81-87393-80-1

Cover Illustration and Design by : Rupambika Khandai
Email: rupambika@gmail.com

Typeset in Adobe Garamond Pro by Arun Sharma,
Akriti Graphic Solution, Delhi-110081 E-mail: arun263923@gmail.com,
Ph: 9999414390

Dedicated to:

Smt. Urmila Batra (aka Santosh Taneja)

This book is dedicated to "MY MAA" who passed away recently after a brave fight with Schizophrenia and Parkinson's for almost two decades. When I started writing this book, it was my fond hope that I would be able to read if not all, at least a part of it to her. I wished to share with her the story of a random man, a man with no roots, no identity and I wished to hear her take on it.

Had she been alive today and had she realized that I had written a book, I know she would have been first very surprised that I had actually written a book and then she would have been intensely proud. It would not have mattered to her if the book was a masterpiece or not, she would have just been happy and encouraged me to pursue all my dreams and go where ever they took me.

MAA, I miss you…

Contents

Foreword

Through a common friend, I came to know about Anoop and his book. Anoop was a merchant navy officer who has traveled the world. Anoop narrated the story. He talked of his concept "a person within a person" with passion and zeal. The tussle between the two personalities, how it shapes, and how it paves the way of life for his central character Neil. After hearing the story of his book, I was sure that anyone would be able to relate to such a story, I could feel that the reader would be able to relate to the deceit, love, betrayal, and pain shown in different chapters of the book.

The book starts at a rapid pace, slows down a bit, and then when you least expect new event develops and engrosses the reader again. The book towards the end gallops along at a very fast pace just like days we all have in our life when life seems to be spinning out of control and you are trying to hold on to your dream, faith, and still march on. For a first attempt, I believe Anoop has depicted the imaginary character of Neil very well. By the time he launches this book, his second book which would be about the life of Ruby would be also coming soon. What I liked most about this book is that it is like a blank canvas with parts left for readers to develop themselves while they read the book and paint their own pictures. One is not restricted by the place, time, or other realities of the characters, and being from the field of art I like imagining and developing my own picture.

Anoop intends to pass the earning from the book to support the treatment/research of Schizophrenia and other such related issues, as this book is dedicated to his mother who passed away a few years back. Mrs. Santosh Taneja was a pillar of strength and an idol for him. Anoop and his family lived through this ordeal for decades with her suffering from it and this inspired him to write this story where an imaginary second half of you dictates and governs your life. I wish him all the success and hope he gets the support for his first attempt and he grows as a writer going forward.

With love n best wishes
RANDEEP HOODA

Word of Thanks

It was only possible with the love, patience & support of my family, and friends that I have managed to complete the book. My wife, my son and my parents have been my inspiration and ardent support during my journey. I would like to thank all of my friends and family who read the various drafts, suggested some improvements, and even helped despite me being stubborn about the plot and how it should develop.

I would like to thank Adroit publishing house for taking a risk with a new author and showing the willingness to publish my first book. A special thanks to Mr. Akhil who stood by me even in trying times of COVID and helped with lot of different aspects.

Dr. Geetanjali Chatterjee former Deputy secretary of Sahitya Akademi who kindly agreed to review the book and provide inputs to improve the flow of the book without changing the original storyline.

Ms. Rupambika Khandai for designing the cover, we went through multiple designs and some of my family and friends were asked for reviews before we finalised the current version. Harshita Gautam, Ravi Patel and Aaklit Taneja also did some last minute changes to the cover and deserve a mention for their efforts. A note of thanks to Mr. Arun Sharma for being patient and helping with multiple iterations of typesetting.

The book is a work of fiction, but it draws from the life's experiences some of which I had seen and some which I heard others may have endured. The characters, instances, and dialogues are purely imaginary with no direct quotes from any person living or dead. The book is an intentional attempt to narrate a story without naming a place or providing background information of characters, I leave it to the reader to develop own background and setting for the book. I always do that while reading a book, I like to imagine what if this was the place the book was set in, so I decided to not describe a place or set up the scene.

I started writing the first chapter about 10 years ago, however after various iterations we were going around in circles and not able to get past the first few pages. But in 2017, I changed my job and, I completed the first draft in 4 months. After which started the difficult and challenging phase to be my own critique, close any loose ends which took more than a year. During which time I lost my mother, and then I lost interest to even pursue this dream. I could not quit after being so close so here is my version of Neil- A random man.

I am indebted to the readers who read this book, they can provide their feedback to me and this will me to get better at the art of writing. See you soon with the second book in the series, "Ruby, the random woman"

THANK YOU EVERYONE and GOD BLESS

Prologue

It is Sunday. Neil opens his eyes, looks around and finds himself in his own studio apartment. The comfort of his own bed brings relief to him. Lately, he has been experiencing some very disturbing dreams. It seemed that he is living a double life….one, which everyone can perceive and another, which only he can feel "within", in his bones. During his sleep and sometimes even when he is awake, he finds himself transformed into someone else who he is not, but maybe he is actually that person. He refers this other persona as 'Sam'.

Today is one of those lazy days when he can just sit back, relax and see the world flow by. The day is bright and clear, not a single cloud in the sky. A cool breeze strongly persuades a person to don something on in order to protect oneself from the harsh, cold weather. He strips away his duvet, stretches himself in bed and lazily reaches for the bottle of water he keeps on his night stand. Taking a few long gulps from it, he walks up to the French window.

He opens the sliding door and steps out on the balcony on bare feet. The ice-cold floor sends a shiver through his body. Soon his feet start to feel numb so he scurries back to the sanctuary of his heated apartment and looks around. All of 35 square metres, his whole life and belongings are in this room except various investments which he has smartly made to yield perks in the future one day. He wonders whether that day will ever come. He walks upto the apartments' open kitchen and fills a kettle with water. The sound of the running water makes him want to go, pee and feel human again. He puts the kettle to boil and walks to the bathroom sloth-like. The bathroom is his den, it is the largest room in his posh apartment. Neil had gone through an excruciating experience to design this studio apartment. The bathroom is his sanctuary from the outside world and he spends a lot of time here. He likes to read while in the bath, listen to music. He even reads the news updates while gracing the throne.

On his day off, Neil can easily spend two hours or sometimes even longer here.. There have been times when he has eventually left this sanctuary smelling like a mix of exotic fruits. His skin flushed from receiving a beating at the hands of the hot shower and his hands looking like shriveled raisins. Neil looks in the mirror and sees a handsome man who does not look a day over thirty; staring back at him, perhaps with just a trace of anxiety. With his grafted, dyed and properly groomed hair and a pampered shining spa face he can give much younger people a run for their money. Neil looks dashing and Sam possessing the charm and the manner of articulation and easy flirtatious abilities, they are a deadly package. He is 50 years old but sometimes he thinks of himself as a 30-year-old young man. This is not something, which only he feels. Very few men actually ever admit or act their age. His thoughts are today roving all over the place and he does not know why. Normally when he wakes up and gets ready for the day, he is well prepared with his day's remarks all catalogued and accounted for. He is a man of careful planning. This habit has sustained him since time immemorial. Sometimes he did not achieve the desired results but he is proud of his prowess to adapt to situations and his willingness to accept change and move on.

1

Thirty- five year old Neil is senior manager in a reputed company. He is "happily" married and lives with his wife and two children in an upcoming suburb. He has a posh house, an imported car and every material object that would make anyone in his circle feel a pang of jealousy. Today, while Neil is waiting for the board meeting to begin, he remembers how Sam few years back stole the idea of his friend and presented it to the senior management and then when his friend Scott tried to claim ownership Sam again helped him to get rid of his friend. Scott was not only a friend, but he was 10 years senior to him and his mentor. He had been a father figure who saw the rare potential in young Neil when he came for his job interview.

> To be honest Neil feels guilty after all these years…Neil is transported back in time…

Scott always told him and anybody else who was willing to listen that he felt a connection that day and therefore decided to grant a chance to a young blue-eyed MBA graduate who was previously rejected by five big companies. After hearing the same story repeated in various ways, Sam developed extreme hatred for Scott. Neil however was ever grateful to Scott and would not listen to Sam. Scott was kind and even generous to provide accommodation to Neil for six months in his house within a week of Neil's joining the company.

One day during the coffee break, Neil was talking about how difficult it was to live in this big and costly city. He was unable to find a small apartment for himself. He was also complaining about people being insensitive and reluctant to rent an apartment to him without a guarantee from the company or a personal bond. Scott told him that he should not worry because he had a spare room in his house. Neil was initially reluctant but when Scott brought up the idea that he can pay rent, Neil agreed.

Neil (along with Sam) shifted into a room in Scott's house. Scott was going to get married in six months so in the meanwhile Neil could look for a place. Neil got along well with Scott's fiancé Ruby who used to drop by at any time at Scott's house. She was a fun loving girl and always ready to party. Scott was on a career high and was destined to become an executive member on the board of the company in a few years or perhaps even sooner. Ruby was not only drop-dead gorgeous but a Miss Trends winner two years back. Scott spoilt her silly and would frequently give into her mostly unreasonable demands.

She had the whole world at her feet but for some reason, loved the company of Scott. No one could figure out why, but everyone talked about it behind their backs. The point of gossip was simple: what an unevenly matched couple they were. Though she was about ten years younger to Scott, she looked more like his daughter than his girlfriend.

Neil was thankful and full of gratitude when he started to work for Scott. They used to spend a lot of time together, and slowly Neil realized that Scott was not the superhero he thought him to be. However, Neil himself was like a lost puppy in this badass corporate world. Scott came from an affluent family and that is why perhaps it appeared that he valued little his achievements or cared for money.

Neil, on the other hand, had completed his studies with the help of bank loans and had financial constraints that he could not ignore. He clutched on to his job with both his hands. Neil did not want to rock the boat but ride the waves and gain the valuable experience before marching on to newer pastures. Some days Neil could overhear long fights between Ruby and Scott. However, Neil just closed his ears to it just as he did when his parents fought. Once over, Scott and Ruby would always kiss and make up. The lovebirds would spend many hours together for a few days until something triggered her to throw a tantrum again. Not that Scott did not lose his cool but he was older, more mature and checked his emotions to present his point of view in a dignified manner.

Once Scott and Ruby had a few friends coming over to celebrate Ruby's birthday. This close group of friends came over regularly, all very posh and chic group. With free flowing alcohol and food, these parties were always a hit. Ruby came dressed in a short dress. A huge argument began to the extent that they almost called off the party. This was even worse since they called each other names, screamed, shouted and even contemplated calling off the wedding.

Neil managed to intervene and got both of them to calm down. Sam used to look forward to these parties, which not only had free flowing booze and food but also some real good looking and glamorous girls. Not to mention, it also provided an occasional chance to hit on some of those gorgeous girls who thought Neil was Scott's younger brother. Some of them possibly thought Neil was a good catch and playfully flirted with him. On one such occasion, Sandra, whom Neil admired greatly, managed to corner him in the kitchen and subsequently took him to the terrace. She stood close and looked at Neil lustfully. Neil placed his hand on her shoulder. She was wearing an off-shoulder dress. It was a bit chilly so Neil asked her if she was feeling cold. She simply turned around, looked at the empty room and on discerning that there was no one nearby, She pressed her cold lips on to his lips and kissed him forcefully. He felt goose flesh on his arms and neck; She murmured your beard is soft and ticklish.

Neil was in a state of shock and did not know what had hit him. He was also a bit nervous lest she reveal everything once they went back. Thankfully, she did not say anything or talk to anyone about it.

Sandra loved to smoke and with no one else willing to give her company, Neil often joined her on the terrace. He once took a drag but the loud and forceful bout of coughing which followed made everyone to rush out to the terrace. Neil, the first time smoker was teased by everyone, led by Sandra who was cajoling him to try it again.

After a month since Sandra and Neil had been engaged in this occasional platonic tete-a-tete, Sam wanted to take over. He wished to do things that Neil would say were not truly moral but on one occasion Sam managed to break free of Neil's shackles. Sam kissed Sandra full on her lips and she responded. Sam being the bold one asked her if they should go somewhere the following day and surprisingly she agreed and even offered to drive.

That night Neil almost died of a heart attack worrying about what would happen if Scott came to know of it but by next morning Sam was controlling him. Sandra drove straight to her apartment and invited him in. What followed was something Neil did not ever contemplate in his wildest dream but Sam was over the moon after having spent the afternoon in bed with Sandra.

From then on, the meetings became a regular weekend ritual. Sandra would come to take Neil to her apartment. Sam did not care about anything but Neil was stuck in the horns of a dilemma wondering whether what he was doing was right. He knew Sandra was a close friend of Ruby and someday it would all blow up in his face.

Sandra calmed him down and told him not to worry. One time while they were in her apartment one of her other friends Sonia dropped in. Sandra had no other option but to invite her in. Seeing Neil there, she winked at Sandra and said, "Now I know why you are so busy nowadays and don't have any time to meet your friends." Together, they joked at the expense of Neil who was wondering how to disappear. While leaving Sandra's house, Sonia pinched him and whispered in a seductive tone "Let us also taste this delicious pie someday!!" Sonia bit his ear lightly and laughed before moving away. Neil hurried out but he could hear the sounds of laughter from the room.

Soon enough Sonia called him and then it did not take long for him to be popular with the other girls of the gang. Sam was enjoying all this attention and also the occasional gifts of expensive clothes and other things. His outlook towards life was fast changing.

Neil had bigger issues. All the promises of hard work he had made to Scott seemed to be evaporating into thin air. His work suffered and he frequently did not make it to the office on time. He had been in the company only a few months, but now Scott was getting a bit impatient. Scott kept picturing Neil as the same fresh graduate whom he met a few months back, not being aware of his hedonistic lifestyle

Little did Scott know that Sam existed behind his back. Sam was now occasionally meeting Ruby, enjoying her company too, and visiting her house too. Ruby too was delighted to add more spice to her already interesting life. Neil who appeared docile and ever obedient in front of Scott was somebody else when he was alone with Ruby.

2

While all these different facets of life were playing their roles in Neil's life, quite unknown to him fate was unfolding and planning his future. Scott and Ruby had started preparing for their marriage in earnest. Ruby had finally managed to convince her parents about Scott being an ideal boy for her. Her parents had resolved their differences with her and were looking forward to the wedding. Scott on the other hand had no success with his parents. His parents, especially his mother, always suspected Ruby to be a gold-digger. Despite all the intense arguments and protests from Scott, his mother refused to give her consent to the marriage.

Scott, without his parents' approval, went ahead and started to prepare for his future life with his beautiful would-be wife. Ruby and Scott spent endless hours planning their dream wedding. She wanted it to be the best wedding ever and kept reminding Scott this. Scott only wanted Ruby to be happy and agreed to almost everything she said or wanted. If it were up to Ruby, she would possibly plan the color of the sky too. She loved to take care of the minutest details and was giving sleepless night to the wedding planner. Her mantra was simple: "If I am going to pay you; you better be at my beck and call to fulfill my wishes".

Every small thing that could be planned was planned. The color of the dishes and design of the cutlery was finally decided after days of debate. Ruby had a certain design in her mind, and the wedding planners kept showing her design after design but she kept on rejecting each one of them for the perfect "wow" one. Matching tablecloths, coordinated reception hall lights, the open area for wedding vows and its decoration with seasonal flowers – all came together.

The menu was possibly another tough decision to take since Ruby insisted on five colors for everything, whether it was for the snacks, drinks, entrée, main course or dessert. Scott initially started calling her tinker bell in private but soon he was saying it loud in front of others too.

While Ruby was busy in her own world, Sam started feeling a bit neglected and occasionally tried to corner her. However, she was always busy and did not have any time for him. He felt hurt and wanted to plan some form of revenge. Neil tried his best to keep insane Sam in check.

Neil was happy because Scott was happy. He was trying to contribute as much as he could because he always felt indebted to him. With the marriage arrangements shifting gears and moving into overdrive, Scott was relying more on Neil to shoulder more responsibilities and take a more active role.

Sam was delighted with all the opportunities suddenly available to him but at the same time, he was upset with Ruby for ignoring him. Sometimes when he was alone he contemplated ways to hurt Ruby but he checked himself when he remembered the fun he was having just because of the marriage. He did not want to miss out on that fun either. Sam wanted these preparations for the marriage to never end. Maybe he should have wished for something else.

It was a cold December night. Scott had gone to his parents' house for dinner, and once again, the topic of his marriage came up. This was a recurring topic for the last six months whenever he came home and it was getting to be quite irritating. He was nursing his second large scotch on the rocks with dad when suddenly his mom burst into the room crying and pleaded with him not to marry Ruby. Scott was initially taken aback but realized he could not take it anymore. He was under constant work pressure and could live without this extra drama in his life.

He excused himself while maintaining a calm demeanor and walked out of his parents' place without having dinner. He sat in his car, let go a loud scream and started taking his frustration out on the steering wheel. Finally, when he could not get any relief, he started the car, and accelerated through the silent streets of the countryside. With hardly any traffic on the road, only the accelerating car was keeping him focused and despite everything, it had a calming effect on him.

Suddenly a flash of light blinded his eyes. Scott did not know if it was an oncoming vehicle or something else: he reacted instinctively, swerved his vehicle, and hit the curb. The car being at a much higher speed than speed limit, lost control and leapt off the ground, and he felt as if he was flying. He saw a tree come up in front of the airborne car and the collision with it stopped the car in mid-air for a moment. Then gravity took over and the car started falling down in a cacophony of different sounds until it came to a rest on the ground with a loud violent thud followed by sounds of metal being crunched and then silence.

Scott's legs were caught in the warped metal of whatever little was left of his beloved car, once his prized possession.

Scott could barely move, one hand was stuck at an awkward angle. With his other hand, he tried desperately to unbuckle his seat belt. Breathing was becoming difficult. He felt himself falling into unconsciousness. The last thing he remembered was taking out his phone and dialing the first number in his call log, crying in a muffled voice, " NEIL…!! HELP..!! NEIL..!! HELP!!"

Neil could not understand what was going on. He knew Scott had gone to his parents house for dinner, and he was also aware of the growing tensions in the family due to the impending marriage. Normally Scott came back close to midnight really frustrated and in a foul mood but today it was only 9.25 pm.

Neil could not shake off the desperate but very weak voice he had heard. His first reaction was Scott or some other friend was playing a prank. After a few minutes, Neil tried to call up Scott but all he got was a busy tone. After trying his number frantically for almost 25 minutes and getting a busy tone, Neil started getting a bit worried. The sound of Scott's last call reverberated in his ears. Finally, after pacing in his room for a few minutes he called up Scott's dad.

After the phone rang for a few minutes, he heard Scott's father on the other end. After sharing the proverbial niceties, he jumped to the main reason of his call and asked if he could talk to Scott. There was a momentary silence on the other end after which he expected to hear a shout, *"Hey Scott, Neil wants to speak to you.."* Neil waited a few more seconds and asked – "Sir, are you there? Can I please speak to Scott?" Finally, Scott's dad gave out a loud sigh and said, "There is nothing hidden from you. You are like a younger son to me. We had a heated discussion about his marriage just before dinner and Scott left without having dinner."

Neil was trying to calculate the travel time among other variables in his head. He asked further, "Can you please tell me tell me what time Scott left? Scott's father said that it was a little after 9 pm and should be arriving very soon there. Neil apologized and wished him good night.

He looked up Google maps for the nearest hospital in a radius of about 30-40 kilometres from Scotts' parents' place. Meanwhile he called up the Emergency services and told them about the call from Scott. He emphasized that he feared his friend was in some kind of trouble. Neil explained that Scott left his house very angry and might be driving under a lot of duress and something untoward may have happened. The lady on the other end was simply rude or in no mood to fill endless paperwork just before end of her shift. She kept repeating that they could not do much and he needed to contact the local police.

He called the local police number and tried to explain his apprehension to them. The constable on duty just laughed and said that Scott might be sitting in a bar on the highway and once he had his fill, he would be back. Feeling frustrated he slammed down his phone with a threat that he would report him to his seniors.

Now he was getting desperate. He knew the password of Scott's laptop so he logged onto it and traced his phone. He saw the phone was still active and placed him about 50 kilometres from his parents place but off-road around 50 metres from the highway. The signal echo was stationery. He picked up his car keys and ran out to his car. He started his car and accelerated off. At the same time, he called up the hospital and asked them to send an ambulance to the spot. While driving at break-neck speed, and simultaneously talking on phone, he narrowly missed hitting a garbage truck right in front of him and ending up in a hospital himself.

He eased off on the accelerator but still kept just above the speed limit. He was still multi-tasking. He managed to get a positive response from the hospital that they were on their way. He called the police station and said straight-away, "I have to report an accident and need urgent help or else someone might die.." Now he got the duty policeman's attention and subsequently gave a graphic description of a badly mangled car and someone trapped in it crying for help and bleeding profusely, etc. Neil hurriedly told them the position of the incident and requested urgent help. After disconnecting the phone, he prayed that all of that was only a figment of his imagination and Scott was okay.

He called up another friend who owned a car garage. The person was badly drunk and incoherent but seemed to understand the urgency and reduced the music volume to listen to him. Neil requested him to get his crew immediately with cutters, crane and come to the crash site.

Now he concentrated on driving but suddenly became aware that he had told everyone there had been an accident. What if they all reached and found nothing had happened? He could not understand how he could describe the incident in such detail and with so much confidence when he did not know anything except the phone call.

Neil started to plan his apologies and what all he would need to do in case there had been no accident. He had a tussle between his brain and heart, as was always the case when he somehow knew that he had lived this incident before. The only clear memory he did not have was if his friend would survive.

The scene from the dream of a car crash he had about three months, came back to him in a flash. The dark cold night and image of a mangled car flashed before his eyes. He could not see the color of the car or even recognize what type of car it was but now he realized that he had actually been forewarned. He had tried to replay the dream a few times just after that but he could not recollect anything. All he remembered was an unrecognizable shadow driving a car, and it was too dark to see where the car was going and he was rushing to the car accident site and on reaching found the mangled remains of the car. After that he could not sleep for days wondering if anyone had survived the crash!

3

Bright lights, alarms ringing, people screaming and shouting, cranes moving, the noise of metal being cut, some smoke rising from the site greeted Neil to the site of the crash. The bright lights, so many people running, moving around gave the impression as if it was a scene from a recent action movie.

The car was already beyond recognition and now with metal and gas cutters working on it relentlessly, it looked more like an experimental mass of metal being moulded or corrected.

Neil tried to have a closer look but was stopped by two police officers who needed him to identify himself. Once he had briefed them that he was like family to Scott, he was advised to wait in his car. The cold words conveyed the last thing he wanted to hear that Scott may not come out alive from this incident. Neil's heart was full of emotions and he felt a heaviness in his chest which made it hard to breath.

A few minutes passed while Neil tried to calm himself and regain his composure. He was wondering if he should call up Ruby or Scott's parents. Right then he saw a familiar van with a dish antenna passing him by. He realized that the decision had been made for him. Rather than the family watching it on the news or worse someone calling them up and telling them about it, it was better that he informed them.

Neil took a deep breath and dialed Ruby's number only to be greeted by her chirpy voicemail – "Thanks for calling, I am busy planning my wedding so please leave me a message, I will get back to you… maybe never". He left a brief message-"Please call me - Neil". He took a deep breath and dialed Scott's parents' residence. The phone kept ringing for a while, and just when he was about to disconnect and try the mobile phone, he heard a sleepy Hello, followed by *"It better be urgent at this hour"* in the background from Scott's dad.

He could only manage "Sorry to call you at this hour ma'am but I only wanted to inform you that Scott had a minor accident and I am with him, once he is able to call you he will". Even before he could complete his sentence, Scott's mother broke into a loud wail, and started to ask to speak to her son and he could hear the heaviness and regret in her voice. Neil was thinking about what he should say when he heard the booming voice of Scott's father, "Who is it?" He replied- "Sir it is Neil and I am with Scott, he had an accident and I only wanted to inform you. Please do not worry if you watch some news on TV."

Upon inquiring about the well-being of his son, Neil was put in a difficult situation. He did not want to lie but could not say the truth either, so he said that Scott was safe and that he would tell him to call later. Scott's father was not fooled by this attempt to divert his query and fired another question, "Where are you?" Neil described where he was leaving out the most graphic details itched in his mind.

He could hear all the commotion for a few minutes that seemed like an eternity while Scott's dad tried to explain to others. Then he only said "I am on my way" and before Neil could even argue or say anything the line was disconnected. Now Neil entered the damage control mode automatically. He knew Neil's parents would be very distraught when they saw the car in this condition. His mind was running all kinds of scenarios while he was trying to pick the best possible option to make the impact as gentle as possible.

His chain of thought was broken by the ringing of his phone, It was Ruby. He wondered whether the night would ever end. He picked up the phone only to be greeted by Ruby coyly asking him- "What is it you want?" Neil was getting desperate and did not feel like talking to anyone and just said, "Scott is badly hurt, get here ASAP. I am sending you the location, Scott's parents are on their way too".

From his distant position, Neil saw the top of the car being lifted by a crane and the right side of the car being cut open. He also watched as the rescue team moved a Neil Robertson stretcher. Nothing he had seen before in his life could have ever prepared him for that sight. The face and the left arm was possibly the only thing which could be recognized while the rest of the body was covered in blood or not visible at all.

A few minutes later the stretcher was put in an ambulance and it left for the hospital. He tried to get a good look at his friend but everything happened in a flash. He overheard the paramedics say that he was still breathing but the blood loss was monumental.

He saw the camera crew talking to anyone who was willing to speak to them. They were trying to identify the victim and make a story of it. Can one blame them for making a sensational news about someone's misery? Maybe Yes and then maybe No...!" He saw a police officer near the barricade pointing towards his direction and the camera crew turning and heading in his direction. He was in no state to speak.

He knew so little about what had happened and how it happened. He just got back into his car, locked himself in it and tears started to roll down his cheeks. He was aware of how persistent news hungry reporters could be. He turned the key in the ignition and eased his car out of its parking spot. He started to move in the same direction as the ambulance. Once on the highway he floored the accelerator. With a squeal of tires and a bit of smoke, he was out of the frame of the camera man who was desperately trying to keep him in focus.

Now back on the road he tried to figure out which hospital they would have taken Scott. He pulled out his phone and called up his car repair friend. He answered but could not hear him so Neil screamed and asked him to check his message. He tried to balance his phone in one hand while trying to type out quickly-which hospital? Once he pressed the SEND button, he waited for a few seconds that seemed like eternity when the screen lit up again read St. John hospital.

He had a good idea where the hospital was but was not exactly sure so he once again tried to fiddle with the GPS Navigator while driving to guide him to the hospital. GPS navigator informed him that he would be there in 10 minutes. It also beeped the warning signal that the speed monitor would be on this route. He looked at his speedometer and he was doing over 110 km/hour, way over the 70 km/hour speed limit on this country road. He eased back his foot on the accelerator for the second time that night.

Neil ran to the entrance of the hospital after leaving his car in the first parking spot he could find. He asked the attendant on duty about Scott, but got nothing from him. They informed him as he was not Scott's immediate family, they cannot tell him. He was getting a bit frustrated, he looked pleadingly at the attendant and said, "Please, I am like a brother to him and only want to know where and what condition he is in, this will give me time to prepare for arrival of his fiancé and old parents". Finally, the attendant directed him to the second floor Operation Theatre.

Neil did not wait for the elevator but ran up the stairs climbing two at a time and was panting by the time he reached the second floor. He made a secret pact to start getting back in shape once all this was behind him.

He saw a bit of buzz outside Operation Theatre 2, and asked the person who seemed to be incharge "How is Scott now?" However, once again, his question was greeted by another question- "Are you family? If yes, we urgently need some blood for him. What is your blood type?"

As luck would have it, Neil was O negative, a universal donor. He quietly mentioned this and headed towards the pointed door to do what little he could to save his friend.. boss... mentor... brother. While being hooked up to the machine he asked again "Can you please tell me how is Scott?" The cute nurse curtly smiled which made the Sam inside him stir. However, before he could make his move, she replied, "I do not have all the details but all I can say is, it is too early to say but God willing he might survive although he would have his share of scars to remember this night."

Sam tried to ask her for her mobile number but she was too distracted and left without even acknowledging his query. This rejection hurt Sam a bit who had started to believe in the last few months that he was invincible and can command any girl to do whatever he wanted and she would do it.

While Sam was scheming his next strategy to win over this nurse by using and portraying how much this tragedy was affecting him. Neil was silently praying for God's help to save his friend. The two very different roles were being played with in him simultaneously; twenty minutes went by while Neil was donating blood for his friends. The nurse was back to take the unit of blood, disconnect the tube and withdraw the needle.

Once again, she professionally and swiftly completed her job while instructing Neil to keep lying down for a few minutes. She left even before Sam could open his mouth. Neil got up from the easy lounge chair and came out to see Scott's parents arriving at the end of the corridor. He took a deep breath and started walking towards them to offer some words of comfort.

Scott's father was a bit composed and looked at him quizzically. Neil could only repeat what the nurse had just told him - "I came only a few minutes ago and I was told that Scott would be ok." Sam the charmer could not resist to add, "they needed some blood urgently and I have already donated". He also asked them to take a seat while he got something hot for them. Scott's dad turned and said a shot of whisky would be best in the circumstances. He then went and sat on the cold hospital chair covered with an array of green plastic cushions.

Neil's thoughts drifted to the story the cushion might tell if it could speak. What all it had seen and endured in this place. He shuddered at the thought of it and walked away looking for a coffee vendor. He asked for four espressos and then juggled his way back holding four cups and trying not to spill any.

What seemed hours later, a person in surgical scrubs came out of the operation theatre and walked towards them. He was still removing his gloves which had a few spots of blood on it, when Scott's mom asked anxiously-"Doctor, how is Scott?" The Doctor answered- "He was seriously hurt in the accident but the rescue team did a great job in removing him without aggravating his injuries. He was transported to the hospital in good time and we have managed to stop the internal and external bleeding. He is stable and under close observation."

The doctor continued that he would be back in a few hours to review the situation and if required, the attendant had his number to call him. He also advised that he did not see any reason for all of them to stay. "Please leave your contact details with the reception and we will contact you as soon as we know more," he added.

While the doctor was walking away, Ruby passed him, decked up as if she was going to a wedding. The doctor could not help but turn around and watch her walk up to Scott's family. This was not lost on Scott's mother.

Before an altercation could start, Neil said to Ruby - "I hope you had no difficulty to find a ride and I am sorry that I informed you so late about the accident". She said - "I came as quickly I could, and after a mini pause added, How is Scott?" Neil replied, "He is out of danger and now under observation. The doctor has told all of us to go home too and they will call us when they know more."

Neil turned to Scott's parents and asked, "How did you all come? Did he drive in this weather?" Once again before anyone could say anything Scott's mom said, "No, he cannot see even 10 meters at night so Scott's sister who has just got her driving license drove us here". Neil asked Scott's parents to follow the doctor's advice to go home. "I will stay, and in case it is needed, I will call you".

Scott's parents and sister left after a few more minutes as his parents could not even sit any longer and appeared tired because not only it was late at night but the evening had been stressful.

After everyone left, Neil asked Ruby, "What took you so long?" Ruby just looked at him as if to tell him to mind his own business and just went to sit on the same seat where Scott's parents were seated a while back. She asked, "Neil, can you please get me a coffee? My head is spinning." Neil looked at her but did not say anything. Seething with anger, he just walked briskly to the vendor again and got a coffee for her.

After drinking the coffee, Neil could see that Ruby was getting restless. He suggested, "You too can go home and I will call you once we get any further news." Ruby replied sarcastically -"Why should I? To give another reason to Scott's mom to argue why I am not fit for her son". And suddenly out of the blue she frisked out her phone and said, "Neil can you click a picture of me?"

Neil was amazed at her transformation. The Ruby who was quite normal some moments ago was now suddenly full of tears in her eyes and looked as if she was in great pain and suffering. After he clicked two or three pictures of her, he gave the phone back to her. Ruby dabbed her eyes and asked Neil – "I hope my mascara is not smudged?" Neil thought to himself- "Girl, get a life, your fiancé is battling with his life and all you can think of is taking pictures and asking about your mascara!"

Neil got a ping on his phone, he opened it and to his surprise, he saw a notification. Ruby had posted a picture with the caption "feeling sad and sorry at hospital". He wanted to ask, "Oh really?" but bit his tongue and kept quiet.

Finally, after another few minutes, Ruby herself said- "Maybe I should go, it is not serving any purpose sitting here, I will come back tomorrow and then you can leave for some time." Naive Neil said, "So you can be here by 0800 hours? I can then rush back, have a quick shower and go to work at 9 am". Ruby gave him a look which could kill anybody with a weak heart, and said "Are you nuts? it is almost 3 am and by the time I reach home, have a shower and get in bed it will be well past 4 am, I need my beauty sleep. The best I can do is to be here by afternoon."

Neil knew better than to argue with her and said - "Ok, good night ..."

After that, Ruby immediately got up, gathered her purse, scarf and walked away with sound of her stilettos going clickety click in an otherwise eerily silent hospital. Neil texted his friends and told them about the unfortunate incident and also requested if anyone could come and relieve him for a few hours next morning so he could go to office and explain the situation to the management.

Finally, he did not realize when exhaustion took over and he must have dozed off because he suddenly woken up with a jolt when his face dipped and touched the ice- cold metal back of the chair. He saw an attendant passing by and asked, "Can you please give me update about Scott?" The resident doctor stopped and said - "Hi, my name is Raghav and I am the doctor on duty here. He is doing well and I would say no news at this stage is good news. Next forty eight hours would decide how much damage his body has suffered and how strong he is mentally to deal with trauma and stress."

Atleast someone had spoken to him nicely. Neil suddenly felt human again and said "Doc, if you have a few minutes to spare can we have coffee and you can tell more." Dr. Raghav smiled and said - "I saw you almost falling over on that seat, you could definitely do with a cup of coffee, let's go and get some."

Neil and Raghav walked towards the coffee vendor. The man who immediately recognized Raghav and also Neil as this was his third visit in the last few hours asked "Another coffee?" Raghav smiled and said - "As always we need the infusion of life lest we fall over..!!" All three of them smiled while the vendor prepared two fresh coffees for them. The vendor asked- "Doctor, some serious case in Operation Theatre 2? This gentleman is here for his third coffee in the last few hours."

Neil was impressed with his power of observation but the doctor said, "Yes dear, you miss nothing, it is a serious case with multiple injuries and hope he recovers soon. Some day when you pass your medical board and are qualified as a doctor you would know what you seek today is a dream full of stress and pain, although it is satisfying when people get back on their feet. Sometimes, however, when you want to help but cannot, it pains you and you have to learn to live with these disappointments". Raghav turned to Neil and said, "Our boy here is a bright students and dreams to be a doctor one day, he works here at night to save some money so that he can join medical college."

Neil who himself has struggled during his college days looked at the boy with new-found respect and told him "Keep the fire alive and you will succeed, believe me this is from a person who has been through it." He gestured a salute and walked away with the coffee in his hand."

4

After some days, Scott woke up and tried to focus his eyes. His head hurt a lot and when he tried to move his limbs, he found that he had no sensation in his body. He seemed not to be able to move any part of his body. He started to panic and could hear his own heart-beat racing. Suddenly an attendant in a white uniform entered, started checking his charts and quickly called out for a doctor.

The doctor arrived and looked at him, smiled and said "Hello!" Scott could not hear anything but he could see the doctor's lips moving. This time the doctor was bending over him and speaking as if he was speaking to a child very slowly….. H..E..L..L…OOO, the words were not heard but Scott could make out from the movement of his lips and his panic increased. Looking at his elevated anxiety level the doctor gave some instruction to the attendant that was lost due to the rapid movement of lips but he saw the nurse move swiftly out of his vision and then reappear with a syringe. She plunged it in the cannula and soon Scott felt himself becoming calm.

The doctor, after having put Scott back under medication, called the head of the department, filled him with the details, and asked for his advice. Dr. Raghav was asked to confirm the status that patient could not hear him but reacted when being addressed. Dr. Raghav replied in the affirmative. The doctor asked him for a few more details and what treatment he had administered and told him that he would be there soon. Meanwhile, he should ensure that the patient does not get too anxious when he comes around next time.

Dr. Raghav came out of the ICU to find Neil looking at him with the expectation of a miracle. He has seen this look every day for so many days now. Dr. Raghav shook his head, put his hand on Neil's shoulder and said- "Be strong my friend, we have a long road ahead of us. As of now, he is extremely stressed so I have put him under sedation but it seems he had difficulty in understanding and hearing me, that could be because he is disorientated and simply in shock. We should be thankful that he is atleast out of the coma." Since the accident, when he saw Scott as a bundle of flesh soaked in blood, things had not improved much. Today through the glass what he could see was a mummified white mass two times the size of his friend Scott with only a little bit more than his eyes, nose and some parts of his cheeks visible.

After a few hours Neil could not resist himself, He opened the door and walked in. He had never been to an ICU before with so many different instruments attached to a single person. Various machines were showing graphs and humming a continuous sound. He glanced over at some graphs and values although he could not make out much. He could see some of them were changing quite rapidly. While he was still trying to observe and absorb all of this, Scott opened his eyes and looked directly at Neil, perhaps expecting him to answer all his questions. Neil would have given an arm and a leg to see his friend sit up and walk out of this place right away.

He said softly, "Hello Scott, welcome back, it is good to see you." Suddenly he could feel Scott getting a bit anxious and some of his graphs shooting up in the red danger zone.

The alarm rang and Dr. Tom told Neil to move a little to the side and he showed a paper with the following words written on it with a marker to Scott's rapidly shifting eyes - "YOU HAD A SERIOUS ACCIDENT AND YOUR BODY IS IN SHOCK". It took a while for Scott to focus on the paper but he seemed to register it. He blinked his eyes rapidly. Dr. Tom changed the paper to his next statement "WE ARE TRYING TO FIND OUT THE EXTENT OF YOUR DAMAGES, YOU ARE BEING SEDATED FOR SHOCK AND PAIN". Scott again blinked his eyes rapidly. Dr. Tom wrote another sheet and turned it towards Scott, "YOU CAN NOT HEAR US BUT YOU CAN READ, DO NOT WORRY WE WILL GET YOU SORTED (with a smiley)!!

It was obvious that Scott was a bit confused. Dr. Tom advised the attendant to give him another sedative injection. Meanwhile, he discussed with Dr. Raghav about their next course of action, in order to check what other possible functions were impaired and to what extent. Dr. Tom who had years of experience in such cases thought it was a case of labyrinthine concussion, it was a temporary condition that would improve as his body recovered and healed itself. However he did not want this to be an assumption so they scheduled a specialist to visit and seek his advice on this case.

Dr. Tom and Dr. Raghav discussed the case at length and their current estimate was that if nothing major was found further, skin-graft and healing of his fractures including rehabilitation could easily take six months before Scott would leave the hospital.

Dr. Tom asked Neil to bring over Scott's parents next day to discuss the course of their son's treatment. Neil requested if he and Ruby could also be present in the meeting, Dr. Tom shrugged and said, "If his parents have no objection, I do not see any reason why not."

Neil wished the doctor a good day and drove down to Scott's house. Scott's sister greeted him and asked him if he would like to have a drink before asking him about her brother. Before Neil could say anything, Scott's father walked in and repeated the same question. He asked about Scott's mom health and was told she had taken it very hard and held herself solely responsible for the accident. She had refused to leave her bed and was suffering in silence. Neil was relieved to see that Scott's father was composed. He had taken over responsibility of the home front too.

Neil conveyed Dr. Tom's message. Neil was economical with the truth about Scott's hearing as somewhere within him, he still believed that this was a minor hiccup and very soon Scott would be able to hear, and would be on the path of recovery.

"Sir, do you mind if Ruby and I attend this debrief with the doctor tomorrow?" Neil asked. Scott's dad deliberated about it for a moment and then replied, "I hope you have not yet told Ruby about this meeting? You are like a son to me and let us keep it within the family for now. You can call Ruby after the meeting. I am sure it is not lost on you that my wife is not a great fan of Ruby and I want to avoid a situation which will make their relationship further strained and condition of my wife worse."

Neil replied- "I do understand it perfectly, I will not tell Ruby now but call her after the meeting tomorrow."

Neil bade them goodbye and asked if he should come and pick them up next morning. "Don't worry son, I can still drive and if not, we have this cute little lady who is more than capable and eager to drive us down. Moreover you live on the opposite end of the town and it makes no sense to drive all the way just to pick us up."

On his way back Neil stopped at the spot where Scott met with the accident. The site still had the scars from the incident. The grass and shrubs looked as if a cyclone had been through that area. Only a few meters away, it showed a perfect country-side full of greenery and life. Neil was filled with rage and he wanted to find something to blame for the accident. He looked around accusingly at the metal berm, the tree. Finally, after a while he shook his head and left.

Neil realized that except for a few hours every day he has not been home at all. He called up Dr. Raghav and asked him about Scott's condition and if he could go home for a while. He would be back later in the evening and he added please do not hesitate to call him if necessary. Dr. Raghav assured him that he would contact him if needed.

Parking his car in the basement Neil came up the stairs to his apartment. He was about to ring the bell but then realized that no one was home. He opened the door and found Ruby sitting on the couch with a glass of wine in her hand. Patrick the photographer she worked with was in the kitchen cooking something while singing. For a minute, Ruby had a shock on her face but then she recovered quickly and said, "We were in the neighborhood and stopped by for a snack after a long shoot."

Neil was wondering why she was explaining so much to him, why was Patrick so cheerful and singing aloud. Ruby shouted out to Patrick – "Patrick, Patrick see Neil is home too, good thing we came over here. He can fill us in on the latest condition of Scott." Patrick shouted back from the kitchen, "Hello (in a French accent) I am cooking some pasta. Do you want to have some?" Then he walked out of the kitchen. Neil had always seen him fully dressed and dapper. He was a little surprised to see his shirt hanging out and his trouser looking hurriedly pulled on. Patrick was bare foot.

Sam suddenly came alive and sensed what had happened. Sam could smell sex from a mile. Sam wanted to dig out more details but a tired Neil just deflected him saying, "No, I am very tired and would rather put my head down for a while before I head back to the hospital."

Neil looked at Ruby and said, "Scott is better than we expected, he came around today and doctors believe he is going to be on road to recovery very soon". Ruby turned to Patrick, winked and said, "See, our schedule brought me luck. Yay! Scott is going to be home soon."

Neil had seen more than he could take. He entered his room, closed the door and crashed on the bed face-down.

When he got up it took him a while to realize that he was lying on his own bed. He opened the door to get some water. He thought he caught a glimpse of Ruby in Patrick's arms but they moved away before he could really focus. The sound of the door and Neil's shuffling feet had possibly warned them. Maybe it was Sam playing games with him. He had some water and heard the sound of the door closing softly. Ruby and Patrick had left without even saying goodbye. He came to the window and saw both of them walking towards Patrick's flashy car but was not able to discover anything that would confirm what Sam was planting in his head.

He had a cold shower to clear his head, changed into a fresh pair of clothes, grabbed a banana from the fruit bowl, blessing the housekeeper ran down the stairs again. He called up Dr. Raghav and enquired about Scott. Raghav said, "I know that you care a lot about him but it has been only few hours since our last call so chill, Scott is sleeping peacefully."

Neil did not tell him he was on his way to the hospital but said thanks and disconnected. He backed his car out smoothly and headed in the direction of the hospital. As the traffic was light, his mind drifted off to the discussion he had with his Human Resource manager that morning. The human resource manager was very sympathetic towards all that he was doing for Scott but also advised him –"Neil, you are quite young and at the initial stage of your career. I know you are very emotional and respect Scott a lot but unfortunately, since you are not his blood relative, the company has decided to decline your request for further leave after careful consideration. You need to join next Monday." adding, "We have already accommodated you for being absent for the last few days but the show must gone on."

Neil wondered whether the HR people had a heart or they were made on a special assembly line with a mechanical pump inserted instead of a fully functional heart which had no feelings and was not compassionate to people's needs. He reached the conclusion they were mechanically developed and did not have any feelings. He further resolved that from now on, he would consider them to be robots and talk to them with a mathematically correct "YES" or "NO" with no accompanying compassion.

He was surprised to see the hospital coming up on his horizon as he did not feel that he was driving for a while but apparently he was. He made a silent wish- "if I don't get a speeding ticket today, I will treat Scott to a beer once he is back home next Friday." He parked his car in the long duration parking and headed for the ICU floor again.

In the last few days, he had become such a familiar face in the hospital that most of the attendants and some of the doctors too thought that he worked here. He greeted most of the people with a nod and kept walking towards the elevator.

Sam had one of his crazy ideas, "What if all these attendants could be a part of his circle of fun?" He knew that he would not succeed with all of them. He had already failed in his first attempt but that did not deter him from imagining the immense potential and possibilities this offered him. He made a decision to start working on it soon.

On reaching the ICU floor, Neil found Dr. Raghav standing near the coffee vendor chatting with the same young boy again. Raghav had not seen Neil but suddenly Neil felt a bit uneasy when he saw Raghav extending his hand and massaging the young boy's hand. Initially he thought being a doctor he was consoling him or giving him some pep-talk. As he drew closer, the touch seemed to be more like a caress. The boy noticed him and said to Dr. Raghav, a bit loudly, "Neil's here." Dr. Raghav removed his hand quite casually and said "Hello".

While Neil was still trying to figure out whether what he had seen was a fact, when Dr. Raghav smiled, coyly massaging his shoulder and said, "Welcome to the club baby, if you want to have a bit of fun, our friend here knows how to please. However, if you want some big boy fun come to me." The expression of confusion and his wide eyes said something which Dr. Raghav read too.

Dr. Raghav a deep shade of red and slightly taken aback said, Wait!, you are not gay? I always felt the vibes coming from you and I thought you too were trying to get close to me." Neil quickly said, "No, Doctor, I am not". He shook his head and walked away. The young boy shouted, "Here is your coffee just the away you like it." Neil did not stop and kept walking briskly. He kept wondering how Sam would have reacted to it. In his heart of hearts, Neil knew if Sam had to react in this situation, he would beat the shit out of the doctor and thanked his stars that Sam had not surfaced.

Thinking in retrospect about the last few days it suddenly dawned upon him that Dr. Raghav probably thought he was gay because he was single and friendly. He had ofcourse never discussed his love life although Dr. Raghav had discreetly asked him a few times. He suddenly realized that the casual brush of hands or standing a bit close to him in the lift was actually Dr. Raghav trying to communicate to him. He had not paid any heed to all those subtle hints which probably was taken as an affirmation.

Neil was not judgmental and he honestly did not care if the person was straight or gay, but he had reacted in an inappropriate manner. He realized that his reaction was downright rude. He walked back to the coffee centre and apologized to Dr. Raghav and the young boy, "I am sorry I reacted a bit rudely as I was in shock I am unfortunately straight" and added with a smile, "But we can still be friends if you guys promise not to try to convert me..!!" At this remark both of them burst out laughing and suddenly the tension lifted. Neil told Dr. Raghav ,"Please do not stand so close to me in the elevator next time", and they all laughed again.

The rest of the night passed uneventfully with Neil resting in the attendant's room and Dr. Raghav busy with his rounds.

In the morning, Neil had a quick shower and got ready, as he was expecting Dr. Tom to be there around 8 am. He knew Scott's dad, an ex-Army man, would be there dot on time. Scott's dad, despite his age, was always impeccably dressed. His shoes always looked brand new. His clothes were crisp and well-ironed. Neil thought that all of it must be a habit from his army days.

He walked out of the room and went for a quick cup of coffee to really wake himself up. After the hot coffee and a chocolate muffin, he was ready for the day.

Dr. Tom walked by, saying "Good morning, young man" and went for his morning rounds without any further talk. Scott's family came after about 30 minutes and Neil took them to the waiting area outside Dr. Tom office. They all sat in silence, each facing a different tussle inside. The faces were too serious and the silence was getting unbearable. Neil broke the silence and said, "I saw Dr. Tom going for rounds a while back, so he should be here soon." As if he had sensed the proclamation, Dr. Tom just walked in, greeted Scott's parents and asked them about how they were doing and invited them to his office.

They all walked behind Dr. Tom. His office was neat and tidy with one wall dedicated to all his professional trophies and certificates. Neil could never quite understand why would someone display all his certificates of accomplishment and accolades on his office wall. He was trying to understand the reason behind this grand display.

He was a little lost in this grandeur when Dr. Tom invited everyone to sit down on the sofa and pulled a chair for himself. Without much further ado, he said, "I told Neil to invite you today so that I can give my best professional opinion about Scott's condition. I would also like to give an idea and time frame for his recovery." Scott's parents were sitting very close to each other. His dad took his wife's hand between his own hands and caressed them lovingly while the doctor appraised them about Scott's condition.

Dr. Tom said, "Scott has multiple fractures and has a bit of blood loss from his other wounds which can be expected from this kind of a car crash." Hearing the words "car crash", Scott's mom stirred a bit, but the doctor continued, "His wounds are all stitched up and after a few units of blood transfusion, his vital signs seem to be stable. He is conscious now after a few stressful days of wait. His pelvic bone is broken in two places and that is going to take time to heal. Scott may need a couple of more operations for some of his other injuries but I think that unless we find something else, he should be back on his feet in about 3-4 months and may need another month or two of rehabilitation to be as close to fit as he was before this accident happened."

Dr. Tom added further, "He has not been able to hear me since yesterday when he came around but I think this is due to trauma and some concussion which I would think should resolve over the next few days. Due to the sudden explosion like the deployment of air bags or his head banging into something, it is possible to have such a hearing loss. We have already done all examinations and found nothing physically wrong with his ears and hearing."

"Scott is extremely lucky to have survived without any serious and permanent damage. It may seem that he has many injuries but things could have been a lot worse. I am quite hopeful that soon we shall shift him out of the ICU into a normal ward in the next few days depending on the results of some more tests and how he copes with the stress."

"Do you have any questions or would you like to know anything further?" Scott's dad was the only one who cleared his throat and spoke - "Doctor thank you for your time and please do keep us informed regarding any further updates you may have. I am sure that my son is getting the best possible attention and care. I am convinced of it after this assessment and under your care he will recover sooner than later."

Dr. Tom smiled and tapped Scott's dad shoulder and said - "He is a strong boy just like his dad, I will do everything I can to make sure he walks out of here soon."

OOO

5

Scott is conscious again. He has been in and out of consciousness a number of times over the last few days. Dr. Tom was right about Scott's hearing insofar that he could hear almost perfectly now. However, Scott was not happy at all and he voiced his discontent very openly. The only people in whose presence he kept his opinions to himself was his parents. He always wanted to prove to his dad that he was a worthy heir to him.

He had no control over his bodily functions. He felt no sensation in his limbs. He could not move his arms or legs at all. He felt like a virus-infected computer who did not do whatever commands are given by his brain. The most embarrassing part was that he had no control over his bowels. The first few days he died every time the hot pale yellow liquid passed into the bag with the attendant just glancing up and smiling encouragingly at him. He felt so small and at a total loss of words to express his embarrassment knowing someone is watching him pass urine and that he could not do anything about it.

Neil felt pity for Scott when he saw him restless and helpless. Sam was not feeling any emotion towards Scott but plotting to see how he could leverage this condition to his advantage.

Scott was getting a bit impatient with all the nice talk with no real improvement in his condition. The only saving grace was that he had no pending work but his new important project was at a crucial juncture. Being a workaholic, he directed his instructions to Neil and had full confidence in him that he would take good care of his work.

Ruby came over every day to fill him in on the latest development from the world of fashion, her modeling assignments and gossip regarding her friends. He did not care for any of it but he sometimes even asked a few questions to show his interest. Ruby gave him a lot of pep talk about how his progress was amazing and how he would soon hit the gym and get back in shape. Scott was however well aware of the different issues that his body would face even after he was discharged included a few skin grafts once he was strong enough. Currently, only immediate and any life threatening issues were being dealt with. He was told that he would be put through the rehab program once he was mentally and physically recovered enough to endure it.

It was not at all lost on Scott that he had a long and difficult path ahead of him to lead a normal life again. Some days, he woke up with nightmares about that fateful night of the incident. He was told that he did not hit any other vehicle but only a tree. The car flying through the air and the metal crunching sound kept him awake at times. He had often thought how different his life would be if that incident did not happen.

He waited impatiently for Neil to come and update him with the latest developments at the office. The Vice President of the new projects Alex Smith was very fond of Scott and liked his out of the box thinking. He had already visited him twice albeit for a few minutes. His words were encouraging-"Son, your chair will be empty and waiting for you, so don't worry and put all your energy in getting up and walking out of here and I will welcome you with open arms."

Scott wished he could do that today. He have had enough of this hospital and all the pleasant people with smiles and comforting words. He longed to go back to his life of immense competition, stress and everyone trying to scramble up the corporate ladder without giving a damn. Although Scott had always been fair and gave the credit where it was due, he knew many other people who had not and would not hesitate to take advantage even out of this unfortunate situation.

While he was still dreaming about his active days at office Neil walked in, and as per daily routine, asked him about his health. Finding him to be a little low in spirit, he tried to give him some office humor about how some of the colleagues were competing to impress the new intern in office and it was truly hilarious to watch her make all these guys dance to her tune.

Neil suddenly got a bit serious and started discussing the new project with Scott. He whipped out his laptop and showed him the plans created by the design team and how he thought they were not in line with the original idea and would cost a lot more to implement. Even Scott was impressed.

"Neil I am really impressed with your independent thinking and how you have summarized all the challenges we have. I hope you do not go to the next management meeting, else the board may get impressed and hire you in my place."

Neil immediately said- "You are a class apart and you telling me that you are impressed shows that this hospital food is not good for you and we need to get you out of here.

However, I do appreciate your kind words. Now if you can at least suggest the next course of action, I can get this project back on track and keep fulfilling our team motto - We do all projects within the budget, before the deadline and exceed customer expectations."

Scott and Neil were deep in conversation for the next few hours. Scott did most of the talking and Neil took down notes. Finally, they had to break the session when the attendant literally chased Neil out and wheeled in the dinner for Scott. She switched on the television and asked Scott if he wanted to watch the business news channel as always while he had his dinner. Scott nodded his head and was once again his spirits were a bit down knowing that she would feed him like a small boy, then clean up and prepare him for bed, with him just lying helplessly there at her mercy.

Scott hated the situation he was in, his helplessness was forcing him to feel desperate at times. He had thought about killing himself but then he could not even do that with no life in his arms and legs. His situation however had vastly improved from his first few days when he could not hear anything and had no control over many other normal tasks. He could now atleast hear and speak. The motor functions of his limbs were still not functional. Dr. Tom had assured him that it was the result of trauma or possibly a pinched nerve but that they will address once they get a few more tests completed to understand the exact nature of the problem. He liked Dr. Tom and his direct and optimistic approach. He told Scott, "You need to stay strong and put in a lot of hard work but if you give your 100 percent, I will also put in my 120 percent to make sure you recover quickly and leave this hospital on your own two feet." Scott would give anything to see that happen right now but he knew it was wishful thinking and that he would not be walking for a few months at least if at all.

While he was debating in his mind regarding what to think about: more work or the happy place, the medical assistant walked in with his medicines and after his routine childish behavior, forced him to have his medicine so that he could sleep peacefully at night and not keep waking up due to severe pain.

Scott and his parents had a discussion yesterday. Mom did not look good at all and Scott asked them to take care of themselves as he was currently in no shape to take care of them. His dad was the pillar of strength for him and mom.

Dad even joked and said, "If you were that desperate to take a break from work, you should have told me. We would have worked something out. you did not need to take such drastic measures." Scott smiled that his father could make light of this situation while his mom looked scornfully with a hint of a faint smile. Although most people did not get his dad's sense of humor, Scott had always worshipped his dad and wanted to be the ideal son.

Once again, the rhythmic sound of various equipment took over his thought process. He heard "beep... beep... beep.." and "tick.. tick.. tick..." and then other stable sounds till he slowly drifted off to sleep.

Scott had a dream about him and Ruby, how they met and how he was smitten by her. He pulled all the stops to impress her. The more he tried, the more she ignored him. Finally she agreed for a short meeting over a cup of tea. Once they sat down at the coffee shop, time stood still. They were chatting like old friends after a few minutes. Ruby knew how to make him comfortable and once he was in his comfort zone he sang like a canary. Ruby did very little talking and kept asking him about his work and where he worked, and what his education background was.

Once they realized it was a bit late they decided to call it a day but with a promise to meet again. Scott was surprised when the next day he got a call from her around lunch-time informing him that she was in the vicinity and would love to have lunch with him. After a few meetings, they were so comfortable with each other that it felt as if they knew each other for years.

It was a real textbook romance; Scott who had never paid much attention to female companions was suddenly madly in love with this girl. They seemed to be together all the time. Ruby often reminded Scott that he needed to propose to the girl or else someone else will and then he would be left wondering why he never said anything. One day Ruby asked him after dinner about his future plans, and Scott without much thought went down on his knee and asked her to marry him. She was surprised by this sudden boldness but agreed. That day Scott took the initiative and kissed her in public. They walked out hand-in-hand and she crashed at his place for the first time. They had a wonderful time together.

All this seemed to be such a far distant past now. Scott realized that it was not even a year ago when he had met Ruby. To be exact, it was only 9 months and here they were about to get married.

○○○

6

Ruby came to Scott's home almost breathless, drunk and in tears. She kept ringing his doorbell persistently. Neil who was a bit tired finally got up and walked out of his room. He was not used to having the doorbell ring in the middle of the night. It was 4 am.

Neil opened the door and Ruby just collapsed in his arms speaking incoherently. He had no idea what she was speaking so he half-dragged and half-carried her inside and kicked the door to close on his way in.

Neil put her down on the sofa, got some cold water, splashed some on her face and handed her the rest of the glass to drink. She barely had a few sips when she threw up not only the water but a brownish spray of liquid which reeked of alcohol. The fountain of spray fell on Neil too who was standing next to her and before he could react, she had another heave and she threw up more liquid this time on the sitting room chair and herself.

Oblivious of all the commotion she had created, she passed out with all the mess around her. Neil watched it all happen and could not decide the next course of action. Finally he walked hurriedly to the bathroom and got some clean towels. Wetting the towels in warm water, he cleaned her up as much as possible and cleaned up the sofa too. He then took off his own T-shirt and shorts and was now standing just in his underwear, feeling a bit awkward. He removed the stilettoes that Ruby was wearing. Marveling at her well-manicured feet, he cleaned them with a towel. Then he leaned over, lifted her up from the sofa, and carried her to the bathroom in Scott's room.

He put her in the bathtub with her clothes on and tried to clean her up. Ruby stirred a bit and said that she wanted to pee. He stopped the shower and helped her to the toilet. When he wanted to go out of the toilet, she implored him not to leave her and kept holding his hand. He tried to get his hand free but by then, he heard the sound. She got up, dropped her clothes on the floor while still holding his hand and headed straight to the bed.

Neil panicked, but was also mesmerized by her beauty. She played with him on the bed roughly and then dropped next to him. Sam was now fully awake and despite repeated protests from Neil he took Ruby in his arms. She responded to his touch and in no time he was consumed by her beauty. In a few minutes it seemed as though a tornado had hit the bed. Finally both lay fully consumed and panting. Sam had never seen this uninhibited side of Ruby, she was like a wild cat tonight and he was pleased to have spend this time with her.

Ruby started to snore gently in a few minutes. Sam was elated that she had chosen him to be with and started scheming how he could make sure she did not leave him tomorrow when she was sober. Little did he know, destiny had other plans..

Between watching Ruby next to him and his mind working in overdrive, Sam fell asleep. Sometime later, he heard a shuffling sound and woke up to a bright sun shining down. Ruby who had also woken up looking at him with a sparkle in her eyes. He asked her if she would like some coffee and she nodded.

Sam got up made some coffee and returned with a tray in his hand. Ruby was still in bed and making no effort to cover herself up. He gave her the cup of coffee and sat next to her. While he slowly with his free hand caressed her shoulders. Ruby glanced at him and smiled. "What can you do to find me next to you everyday?" For a moment Sam was terrified how she could read his mind but before he could answer, she said, "I will tell you." She told him about her plan. For a moment he was aghast and felt scared of her. But he knew that if he played his cards well, he could gain a lot more than her in his bed. He nodded his consent.

Having agreed to be her partner in crime, Sam felt himself equal to her. Little did he know that Ruby would never consider him her equal or reveal him her whole plan and was busy making her own plans. They agreed to be in contact every day in order to update each other of their progress. They decided not to use any telephone, emails, or other technology where any record would be stored or traced to their alliance. The plan was to meet at Scott's house every evening. Sam already was planning to reap a few extra benefits too.

Ruby now set out to put her plan into action. Sam kept lying around in bed day-dreaming before Neil came alive and cursed himself for not going to work. Sam just disappeared smilingly. Neil got up and took a quick shower cursing himself for letting Sam surface again. He knew that if Sam got control of the situation, it would be the end of him and that he would forever be a slave to Sam. He never admitted but he was afraid of Sam.

Neil left for office but today it was Sam who entered the office. He had decided that it was high time he did something to ensure that it was he who was in control and not Neil. He began by smooth talking to the girl at the reception and enquiring how she had been and what she did in her spare time. The girl always found Neil attractive but hesitated to speak to him thinking that it was not right to be involved with a colleague. The charm net that Sam had cast had caught the right fish. After a few minutes, he carefully introduced gossip that he knew she loved. He casually remarked, "Just between the two of us, Scott is not doing very well and his road to recovery will be hard and long. But don't tell anyone that I told you."

The girl was elated because she not only got to talk to Neil but now they shared a secret too. Little did she know that Sam was using her as a pawn to spread the news about Scott.

Next Sam walked into Vice President Alex's office to update him about the plan discussed between Scott and Neil albeit with a small change. He was going to present it as his own idea. He had planned slowly to sideline Scott or any reference to him. He went in for his scheduled debrief and mentioned Scott only in passing. He said, "Yesterday Scott was a bit tired so I did not stay with him for long. However I worked on the project and have worked out a possible resolution." Then he repeated what Neil and Scott had worked out last night.

The Vice President Alex seemed impressed and complimented him for his hard work. He further added how quickly he had progressed with understanding the company business. Alex's praise boosted his confidence. Sam casually proposed to shift some of the important files from Scott's room to his office. His office was small and being a shared space maybe, it was not a good idea. He hastily added that of course Alex need not bother about these things and that he will keep shuttling between offices although it might affect his work efficiency. He inwardly smiled he had cleverly planted the seed in Alex's mind that he should shift into Scott's office by casually mentioning it.

He managed to further add all the buzzwords, which the Vice President liked and had talked about in the past knowing that this would get him a temporary seat in Scott's office. He would later work on other plans to make it permanent. Alex thought for a few seconds and then said, "I do not see the reason why you cannot install yourself temporarily in that office and once Scott is back, you can move back to your own office. I am sure Scott being the smart and intelligent person that he is, will understand. I suggest that you do not get used to that beautiful office as Scott is going to be back sooner than we all think. He is mentally very strong and he will jump over these small hurdles."

Sam echoed the sentiments as Neil would have done, "Scott is my mentor and I would never be able to take his place. I am going to feel privileged and honored to be able to keep the chair warm for him. Many thanks and I shall get going now. As per our discussion, I will issue orders to the site coordination team to ensure that we economize and fast-track this plan rather than go forward with the project team idea."

Sam entered Scott's office and sat in his chair, looked at the mahogany desk and remembered the day when he had come for his interview as Neil. He remembered being impressed with this office and today he was sitting at the same desk. If someone would had asked him how many years he would take to sit in this chair, he would have answered probably close to a decade or maybe more. However, Ruby and a bit of luck had fallen his way and here he was sitting in this chair.

Sam picked up the desk phone on Scott's desk and dialed the site team. He got the project manager online and said, "Hey, Neil here, I have discussed with Alex, our Vice president the plan and he agreed to make some changes. I am sending you the details that already are approved by him so please take care to implement them as soon as possible. Also if you need any help in Scott's absence feel free to contact me and I shall engage with different people at HQ to get you a desired outcome."

The project manager never really liked being dictated regarding how to run his project but he had no desire to force his opinion if the Vice President and others had already approved the changes.

Sam forwarded the changes to the project manager in the email and cc-ed the Vice President on it, with a remark that as per his discussion with the Vice President that morning, they should find the changes they had to implement in the email attachment. He added, "If you need any clarification or help please call me or send an email to me. This, being an important communication, I have copied the Vice President on this email. However, you need not copy him in your replies and I shall keep him informed. Please acknowledge the receipt of this email and your compliance." For further impact he added in his email signature Company representative. Now with the first act of stamping his authority on the project manager, Sam was looking forward to rein him in and keep him under a tight leash.

Sam started to look at the different sketches and notes on Scott's desk. He found some excellent ideas, which he collected and kept aside, and the rest of the papers were put in two boxes for Scott to deal with when he returned. He had already decided that he was not going to leave this position even if Scott came back. He did not know if his plan would succeed but he knew that with Ruby's help, he would get favorable results.

He copied the sketches and plans he had kept aside on his own laptop and then shredded them so that no one could find them later. Now officially, he was the owner of these documents and he wished to use them to his advantage.

Neil had to plan his next move in order to impress the board in the forthcoming meeting. Sam had learnt of this meeting only today but he knew that he would be invited to represent Scott's work. He did not intend to represent anyone but himself. He smiled to himself and started making a list of things with which he would need help from Scott. He had kept an account of the current issues with the projects and the new project's draft report, which could be the key to impressing the board.

Scott knew about all the projects like the back of his hands but Sam had other interests, which he wanted to take care of now rather than becoming a workaholic like Scott. He knew that he could not dazzle on his own but he knew how to use others to show him as a shining star.

The company was a medium-sized construction company with about 1000 people working there and he was now in a position to be in the top 1 percent of the company although only temporarily. Sam wanted money, fame and a comfortable life like any other man, however, he wanted it quickly and did not want to put in hard work for it.

Sam went to the coffee room and sat down with his colleagues trying to show that nothing had changed. Some of them congratulated him and even demanded a party for his promotion. He tried to show that it was not a big deal and kept repeating that this was only a temporary phase and soon he would be coming back to his old place. He was feeling proud on the inside and wanted to tell each of them to be ready for new shocks every few days but all he said with humility was- "The Vice President asked me to take this office for a few days to resolve the project issues with Scott's help."

He smiled and left when he saw the receptionist enter. He knew that she would definitely share Scott's condition with them and then most of them would add their two bit to it and the company rumor mill would start grinding. He paused for a few seconds at the door to make sure she was whispering what he had told her about Scott to the others. Assured, he smiled and left.

Sam thought that he was in control of the situation and he was the one driving it. He spent the whole day trying to put his mark on various plans and documents using Neil's hard work and Scott's intellect, which he had brazenly taken in his possession. He was not ashamed to be doing what he was doing because he had no shame. He only knew that he wanted to be at the top as soon as he could. The end was more important than the means.

OOO

7

Sam could see that he had got his chance and decided to use it well to achieve his goals. His next plan was to be seen as a hands-on manager. Although he hated fieldwork, he decided to play the role well. He invited the contractor who was the representative of this new project to accompany him to ensure that the plan made was well understood and implemented properly in the field.

Next day, after the morning briefing, where once again he just parroted whatever knowledge he had gained from Scott, Sam left office and went to the site. He met the project manager there who was surprised to see Neil arrive unannounced, Scott gave him a heads up before he came to the site and never came to the site unannounced. He did not quite like Neil coming to the site; however, he had no choice but to engage with him.

And while they were discussing, the project manager was surprised to see the contractor's representative walking in. He did not expect to see him at this hour. The guy came straight to Sam and said, "Good morning and thanks for inviting me, we value our relationship with your company a lot and would do our utmost to ensure that you are a satisfied customer as has been the case for so many years. Without putting any blame on anyone, I would say your plans have been well received and although we may be a day or two behind schedule, we will try and catch up and complete the project before time."

The project manager did not appreciate his job being taken over or rather bypassed. However, he did not want to create an issue and decided to speak about it to Neil later. He was sure Neil would understand his viewpoint and consider it.

The contractor's representative and Sam walked around the site for a while. Sam tried to demonstrate his authority that now he was the boss by pointing out minor things, which normally happen in large construction sites. A small change here or there. After spending an hour with the contractor, Sam told him to meet him on Friday afternoon for a weekly briefing. This was news to the contractors representative but he did not want to say no to his new company representative but he wondered why it was on the friday.

Sam knew that this was one of the biggest contracts the company had and if he played his cards right, the others would be easy to manipulate. He also felt having rescued the project already as he was under constant observation of the Board. Neil did this as he thought it was good for the company, Sam knew it was good for him.

Sam spoke to the project manager after the contractor's representative left, to speak to his site supervisor and told him - "You need to maintain a better control over the contractor. I have arranged regular meetings with the contractor's representative and I would expect that you come to my office every Friday morning too and update me on the latest progress and clear any concerns which we might have."

The project manager was not used to this kind of baby-sitting and prayed in his mind for Scott to return soon and take over his job. He could detect the inexperience and immaturity of Neil within the first few hours. He was an old hand and had seen many managers and general managers of projects. Some were very good, some were not so good but all of them were willing to use his experience to their advantage but so far he had never seen anyone who was as authoritarian as Neil.

Sam left the site soon after and thought he had managed to put his stamp of authority on the project manager and the contractor. The reality was that he had alienated both of them quite a bit. He started formulating a speech in his mind, which he would deliver to the Vice President next morning to brief him about site supervision being slack and how he had managed to get everything under control.

Sam started thinking about how to get information that was more useful from Scott too but not to give him any useful information. The issue was that in order to get information from Scott, Sam would have to give the reins into Neil's hands and Sam did not like it. He was now getting into a power struggle with Neil and wanted to assert his supremacy and show Neil what he could achieve.

Sam did not want to go back to office so he headed towards the hospital. He knew further sound bytes and brownie points were waiting for him there. He saw Scott's parents' car there and was wondering if Scott's sister would be there. He quite liked her but she was not interested in Neil. Sam had tried a few times to strike a conversation with her but either Neil did not let him have his way or she would make an excuse and get away.

He parked his car and went to Scott's room. His parents and sister were sitting there. Neil greeted them and enquired about their well-being. Turning to Scott's sister, he asked, " How are you doing?" After he was done with the pleasantries, he looked at Scott. He could make out that something was not right.

He asked Scott, "Anything wrong?" Scott's dad said that the doctors had done further tests and examinations. They now believed there was some nerve damage and this was the reason why Scott could not use his arms and legs. They surmised that they should be able to treat it with an operation to relieve the nerves being compressed. However it was a tricky operation and there were chances that it could make his condition even worse. Scott would need at least a few rounds of skin grafting to repair the damaged skin tissues and now this further complication meant that he would have to be here for a little while longer. He would need to tell Ruby to postpone the wedding plans for at least another year.

Scott said - "Dad I think you and mom should head home, I do not see how your presence can help anything. Neil is here and we will discuss some official work. It will help to take my mind off this new situation." Scott's parents and sister stuck around for another half an hour. However, the stress and tension in the air was palpable. Finally, Scott's dad said, "I think we should head home before it gets too dark."

There was silence for about ten minutes after they left, while Neil waited for Scott to say something. Scott had his eyes closed but Neil could feel he was seething with anger. Neil was about to say something when suddenly Scott cried out loudly and said, "I hate my life and I hate everything. Can you get me something to end my misery?"

At that moment, not only Neil, but also Sam, felt sorry for him. The person who was so full of life and always told others how to overcome their hurdles was now being a coward and wanted to end his life. Neil told Scott- "I know you and this is not you but your desperation and frustration speaking. I am sure once you think calmly you will realize you do not want what you are asking."

Scott again looked at Neil and laughed- "What I want is to die, I am a vegetable who can speak, who can eat but has no control even over his own bloody bladder!!" The recent events had hurt Scott's ego as he felt his image as a strong leader was disappearing. Scott further added, "I am reduced to an item of display, people come speak to me as if everything is going to be okay when everyone knows it is not, especially today. Can you believe Neil- I may never be able to leave this bed. I may always need an attendant to do even basic daily chores, I need to ask someone to feed me, to fetch me a glass of water and sometimes I fear if I drink more water I may pee more and what will happen if the attendant's schedule is messed up and the urine bag fills up."

Scott kept venting his inner feeling, "Can you imagine what I wish to do, I want to choke myself. The irony is I cannot even do that." and then Scott started to lament and moan loudly. Hearing the commotion, the attendant came running and noticing the erratic spikes on the graphs gave a sedative to calm him down. Eventually Scott drifted off to sleep.

Neil felt like staying until he woke up but the attendant told him that he would not get up for a few hours. Sam started to feel a bit frustrated. He came here to get some bright ideas and now he was left with a lifeless body and no chance to get any further sound bytes. He asked the attendant if Scott was like this from the morning. She said – "No, Scott seemed quite happy this morning, he listened to the news and then asked me to show him some Power-point presentation on the computer, and then he recorded some messages on his phone. After lunch, Dr. Tom came to talk to him and his parents as he had figured out what was causing this shooting pain for last few days in his back and head."

Voila! Sam got his answer, he thanked the attendant and said that he would like to sit with his friend for a while. If she wanted to go for a coffee or take a small break, she was welcome. He would call her if anything was needed. She thanked him and said that she would be back in five minutes after calling her mom, who was little tense due to heavy rains and flooding in the village.

Sam took Scott's phone and opened it. He knew his password. He saw a 35 minutes recording today and a few other recordings. He transferred the recording to his phone and deleted them from Scott's phone. Once it was done, he switched off Scott's phone but then he thought of checking the messages.

Switching on the phone, he saw 10 messages and a few emails. The messages were unread so he quickly forwarded the messages to his phone and deleted all the unread messages. Not taking any chances, he deleted the forwarded messages to him too. He then quickly forwarded the emails to himself and deleted them from Scott's received and sent folders too.

Lastly, he emptied the deleted emails from the deleted folder too. Sam switched off the phone and kept it on the bedside table. He wished Scott all the best in his next life and a quick passage to heaven. He smiled to himself and was happy with all the information he had managed to retrieve today.

He dropped in the chair but was soon feeling restless. He wanted to go home quickly and listen to all the recordings, read the messages and then make his future strategy from the new-found information. He thought leaving immediately may raise some suspicion. After a few minutes, he came out of the room and gestured to the attendant that he was leaving and without even waiting for her to return, he started to walk towards the lift, lost in his own world.

Dr. Raghav who was just coming on his night duty, passed him and then walked back to touch his arm and say "Hey Buddy are you ignoring me?" Neil looked up and apologized. "Scott is not feeling too well with the news of some delay in his recovery and this got me a bit distracted. See you tomorrow. I have got to go now."

Immediately on reaching home, Sam opened his cell phone to listen to Scott's recording. He was astonished to hear Scott speaking so calmly and clearly. The clarity of his thoughts and how much wider his horizons were despite being in pain and such a difficult situation made Sam feel a bit angry. For his whole life he had played second fiddle to someone.

He had to listen to the recording a few times to memorize them verbatim. However, understanding them and being able to use them in the right context would be a bigger challenge. The best part was that Scott had recorded his views with slide numbers so that Neil could refer to it during his presentation but now Sam was the one who was benefitting from it.

Finally having finished writing his notes, Sam felt that his day was really well spent. He then looked at the messages, found nothing really important in it, except one from Ruby where she once again declared her love for Scott and wished him a speedy recovery. Sam could not understand why she was doing this.

He got up, opened a bottle of Scotch, poured himself a stiff one and drank it straight. The whisky burned his throat but soon he was lost in weaving his dreams. He did not realize he had finished half the bottle of Scotch. Finally, he staggered to his room and crashed on the bed.

Sometime later he got up with a dry throat, walked to the kitchen, drank some water directly from the tap, and again staggered back to his bed. He had a beautiful dream that he was getting married to Ruby, and she was whispering "I do." when he woke up to realize that it was just a dream.

He tried to go back to sleep again but sleep eluded him so he once again looked at his phone. It suddenly occurred to him he had not checked the emails which he had copied from Scott's phone.

He opened his email folder to read the subject lines to see if any of them were of any real interest to him. He saw an email from the project manager to Scott, complaining about Neil's behavior. He was infuriated and decided to get rid of this man, before he put any more roadblocks in his way. He thought of a plan but with sleep still not coming his way, he had another few swigs of Scotch straight from the bottle and then dropped on the bed.

He was woken up by the alarm on his phone. He snoozed it and tried to go back to sleep. All of sudden the doorbell rang. Hurriedly donning his pyjamas he opened the front door to find the housemaid standing outside.

She apologized and told him that she had forgotten her house keys here. He waved her in and told her to make him a cup of black coffee. He walked across and laid back on the bed. Few minutes later, she came back with the coffee, left it on the side table, picked up the littered clothes, and the almost empty bottle of scotch while mumbling something in her local dialect.

He told her to go somewhere else and mumble. Finally he got up as he did not want to miss the opportunity to shine again today. He downed the coffee hurriedly though it hardly helped with the massive hangover. He swallowed a few Alka Selzers and had an ice cold shower to wake himself up fully. He shaved quickly but in the hurry nicked his left cheek. Blood started to ooze out. Letting out a curse, he took a large swab of cotton, pressed it to his cheek and waited for the blood to clot so that he could get dressed and leave.

Finally, with the help of cold water and keeping the wound compressed for a while, he managed to stop the bleeding but the gash on his cheek looked ugly so he put a adhesive bandage on it. Dressed in a freshly ironed shirt and his favorite blue suit with a red tie he had a hurried breakfast. The house cleaner had made some eggs and toast for him even though it was not part of her duty. She was supposed to clean and do laundry three times a week for 3 hours each time but seeing his morning state she probably took pity on him. After breakfast he thanked her, left some cash for her kids on the table and went towards his car.

He was supposed to drive straight to office but on sudden impulse he decided to take a quick detour via Ruby's house. He wanted to understand what her plan was a little better. She opened the door and asked him straight up - "Hey, are you checking on me?" The usually cool Sam too was a bit flustered. It seemed that she could read him like an open book.

"I wanted to talk to you about the plan and see if you have developed it any further." She said, "Don't worry, I do not need to plan, things normally fall in my lap." He admired her for a few more minutes and shared some other small talk. He too was not going to lay all his cards on the table until he knew what her cards were. He got up to leave; she passed him and brushed her hand on his thigh. It was as if an electric current had passed through his body. He quickly gathered himself and left before he could lose whatever little control he possessed.

Once outside he lit a cigarette to clear his head of her scent and get ready for the morning meeting. He realized that it was not a good idea to meet her before an important meeting. She distracted him and caused him to lose his train of thoughts. He got into his car and drove away rehearsing his speech on the way.

Sam arrived at the office and rather than parking in the general parking lot, he parked his car in the spot reserved for Scott. Getting out of the car, he straightened his tie, ran his fingers through his hair and moved towards the lift.

He went straight to Scott's cabin, opened his notebook and read it once more to ensure that he understood what all he was going to say and walked towards the conference room. He was a few minutes early and others had not arrived yet. Rather than sitting and fretting he went to the adjoining kitchen and made himself a black coffee, extra strong, to give him the kick-start he needed this morning.

While he was finishing his coffee and moving back to the conference room, he saw the Vice President enter. He wished him good day and then informed him about the setback in Scott's situation with an exaggerated account of Scott's depression and how badly the whole family was hit. He reiterated that he was deeply sorry for them but he was ready to give all the support from his personal time since HR had told him not to miss any more office on this account. With a straight face he added that he did not mind doing it for Scott who was his mentor and someone who had looked after him.

The Vice President said that he was not aware of any decision of the Human Resource department and added, "The discussion was about you taking a few days off without informing anyone. I was not aware that this was because of Scott. However, since the human resource manager was very insistent, I told them to inform you that in future you are not to take any leave without informing your supervisor. I did not know they were making a case out of this recent incident. I will talk to them and we all need to give full mental as well as emotional support to Scott to ensure he can recover quickly. I too am guilty of not being able to visit him."

Sam immediately said, 'I am quite aware how busy you are, and I will convey your wishes to Scott in person today evening itself and if you are okay with it, I can keep you updated on his latest situation more frequently."

By now, the others had started streaming in so the Vice-President only nodded and said, "Okay, do that, and thanks for being a good friend and a caring colleague." Sam too moved to Scott's spot on the table, waiting to see his own name in the near future instead of Scott.

The meeting started with the opening remarks by the Vice President, which made everyone aware of Neil's temporary position in place of Scott. This was followed by the HSE (Human, safety and environment) presentation on safety and other issues. Neil was only observing the others. He saw that almost everyone had their laptop or iPad open in front of them and no one was really paying attention to the person presenting the topic.

He took a few notes and asked the questions which Scott had prepared for different presentations. Once Safety and Finance had given their presentations, it was his turn to speak. He said- "Good morning, I know all of you are very busy and possibly got more important things to catch up with. I am only here as a stopgap and I will be short and quick. However, I request you all to please show some interest in what I am presenting. The site operations are where we can make huge improvements and make this company more profitable."

He heard a few mumbles and disgruntled words from the senior managers. He quickly added, "I know this may not be what you are used to but please bear with me for fifteen minutes and you will see that it will be very interesting and worth your time." He saw most of them close their laptops and some even open their writing pads to take down notes.

He gave a crisp presentation based on Scott's last evening's recording, and wrapped up the meeting with an exaggerated account of his own visit to the site and how he saw some safety and construction lapses, which he had already handled with the project manager. He also commented that he was going to the site at least once every week to ensure that the project manager kept the site proper. Without naming Scott directly, he said that the project management was not being handled properly.

He thanked everyone for their time and moved back to Scott's allocated place. The Vice President clapped first then he was joined by a few others and followed by almost everyone in the room giving him a standing ovation. The Vice President waited for other presentations to be over and then he said as the closing remark, "I am really pleased with Neil's first presentation which was extremely well scripted and he delivered the relevant points to update all of us in a passionate and lively manner. Let's all make sure the young man is set up for success in this interim role for now and then he grows to be an important part of this company."

Neil was elated to hear this praise but this was not his glory. No one but he knew that Sam had stolen it from Scott.

Neil felt he had cheated and was scared. "What if someone got to know how Sam got all this information, what if Scott were to get wind of it?" Sam was out to ruin him and he had no control over him. The more he tried to keep Sam on a leash, the more violent he got.

Neil had at times been scared of Sam but now in the last few days, Sam had become even more dangerous and Neil had to find a way to get the control back. He did not know how he would do it but he should and he would.

With this resolution made, Neil walked back to Scott's office and suddenly he saw the drastic changes his life had undergone with Sam being in charge. Neil was torn between right and wrong. He did not know how to resolve it but he knew one thing that if he did nothing he would be dead and Sam would take over his life.

The phone rang; it was the site manager informing him of a serious accident on site. A worker while working on the 7th floor had fallen down and was unconscious. The worker was being rushed to the hospital but before the news broke out the site manager thought it best to inform him. In today's digital age, it would not take too long before the media hounds were all over the place looking for gossip, news and views from one and all.

Sam was furious, he thought this was due to the site manager being incompetent and he called up the Vice President to inform him about the unfortunate incident. He also assured him that he would personally take care of the matter.

He left the office and went straight to the hospital. He met with the family of the injured worker. He gave them some cash right away and promised to take care of the family with compensation and give his son a job. He urged, begged, pleaded with the wife of the worker to not talk to the media unless he was present to handle it.

"If you talk to the media, we cannot help you and you will have to be on your own." She was too distraught but the money sealed the deal. She had not seen money equivalent to ten days salary in one go. She knew that she had to take care of her four children and if one of them were assured a job, which he had not been able to secure despite running from pillar to post, she would keep her mouth shut.

Sam pulled the son aside and told him softly, "I will give you an office job and even field work like your dad but you need to make sure that this matter is not raised in the press. Come and see me in my office tomorrow or whenever you can."

Both the mother and son promised him their alliance and he was relieved. Next he met the doctor and told him that the company would foot all the bills but no news of his condition should leak out. "Do what you need to do to communicate that worker is well and unless any complication happens he should recover in a while."

Despite all the damage control done by him, some section of the media got scent of it and reported the correct story but most of the other channels and reporters were taken care of by him either by calling them or by not getting the correct picture due to his immediate actions after the incident.

Media has a limited time and interest in this story with only some news channels showing it as a minor injury and routine industrial accident and the matter soon fizzled out. The death of the poor worker was not even reported in any channel.

Sam got his son a job as promised and packed off the whole family to a different town. Some nosey parker reporters did try to make news of it again but he managed to get it all buried.

Sam might not have the intellect of Scott but he was cunning like a fox and he used his skill to gain maximum popularity with the management and board. Some of the Board members who had heard some facts did think that it was a wrong way to handle things but Sam glossed over the details and every time this topic was raised, he managed to divert it to something else.

Sam was now planning an exit strategy for the site manager. He managed to convince the investigation committee of his lies and cover-up. The safety culture at the site was lax due to the site manager not paying attention to detail. The site manager was made the sacrificial lamb in this case and he being an honest person with some conscience anyway blamed himself for the accident. He was let go and Sam installed someone whom he could trust in his place.

Neil was now seen as a genius by most in the company and almost the whole board was impressed with his work. Not many knew how he did it but the results spoke.

He had managed to get the information of progress from various sites routed only to him and he started reporting to the company board and management what they wanted to hear.

In the board room the success and improvements made on different sites were being reported, whereas actually things were quite different. However, the company reputation made people hesitant to speak against the decline in company sites. Either some of the people who tried to raise their voice were sidelined or Sam got rid of any detractors.

The work was done, the board and the management were oblivious of the various other issues brewing, including the mercurial rise of Sam. He was given the interim responsibility to manage the role of Scott; however since he took over, he had only cemented his own position with no regard to how he achieved it. He used all the tricks in his bag to get information from not only Scott but from other people within the company and show it as his own.

The Human Resources manager tried to warn the Vice President about the boisterous behavior of Neil but the management was impressed by the excellent handling of the accident on site and did not want to hear anything against him. Sam was aware that this current situation gave him some advantage and he did everything possible to make the best of the hands he had been dealt with.

8

Scott was feeling a little left out and tried to ask Neil about what was going on in the office. Neil assured him that all was well at the different sites and that he would keep him fully informed of any issues whereever he needed guidance. Scott was not at his 100 percent and sometimes he did feel like he had recorded his thoughts but when he referred back to them, he could not find them. Little did he know that Sam was checking his phone and taking out all he could without leaving any trace.

Scott was getting depressed with no real progress on his physical improvement. He felt dejected, temperamental and moody most of the time. His only solace was work, which too was slowly being taken away by Sam.

Scott did not know and had no idea how badly he was affected by all this manipulation. The medical attendants and doctors could feel the change in Scott's condition over last month but could not pin-point why there was such a drastic change. Scott was seen as a patient with a strong will power but lately it seemed that he had given up on life.

Dr. Raghav and Dr. Tom had frequent discussions as to how to tackle this, with his cast coming off the next week after 8 weeks. They hoped physiotherapy would help in getting some flexibility in his limbs and thus encourage Scott to once again start devoting his energy in the right channel. The current negative mindset was a cause for concern. Dr. Raghav spoke to Neil too about this situation. However, Sam tried to dismiss his concern saying that Scott would be okay soon, and this was only temporary and he had seen him in good spirits at times. Dr. Raghav was not fully convinced but he believed Neil knew Scott better and he too was fooled by the concern and false support shown by Neil for Scott.

Ruby too dropped in to see Scott a couple of times a week. However she was too wrapped up in postponing wedding arrangements and with her own modeling career to really care about Scott. Scott was quite disturbed by how she could only think of herself. He even told her a few times that maybe she should move on as he was not going to leave this bed anytime soon. She showed her false angst at him for even coming up with this ridiculous idea. Although within her heart, she was the one who had worked on getting this notion into his head indirectly in their talks.

Ruby seemed to be getting her plan in action, slowly getting Scott not only frustrated with her but making him the person who wanted her to move on! Sam was working on getting the distraught factor to such a point that the volcano of frustration within Scott would erupt any day.

Scott was also frustrated with Neil for not discussing detailed information from the site. He wanted to know details of the accident on the site, as to how it happened and how it was resolved. Neil never supplied him adequate details regarding it.

Sam and Ruby had systematically cut off all his communication channels with work and friends. Scott could not talk to his parents about his frustration and tried to put up a brave front whenever they visited. It was getting increasingly difficult for him to continue putting up this brave front.

Finally the cast was taken off and Scott was surprised to see how much his limbs had shrunk in the last few weeks, but he was still worried about not having any ability to control them. The doctor had advised Scott that physiotherapy would start next week. Meanwhile another round of plastic surgery was planned to restructure his left ear lobe and a part of his cheek.

Dr. Tom and Dr. Raghav discussed the various options they had. They knew some nerves were being pinched and wanted to consult a neurosurgeon to see if this could be solved to help with getting Scott's limbs back to life. They had already had a few discussions with the medical council and experts in neuroscience about Scott's case. However, given his original severe injury the advice was to get his immediate injuries attended to first and then move on to other things.

Dr. Raghav after their discussion booked another meeting with the medical council and the neuroscience department to see how to tackle the case. He and Dr. Tom decided that it was good to involve a psychologist too. Sometimes they could come up with solutions which medical science struggled with.

Scott had the operation for restructuring his left ear lobe and cheek. Although still in bandages, his face seemed and felt to be little more symmetrical to himself. He was explained that all this reconstruction was time consuming and it would take several months and possibly a few more minor operations.

Physiotherapy was quite demanding and draining for him. He did not like being touched but he had no say in it. Scott liked his personal space and currently his space was being violated which made him uneasy and unhappy. He waited for the massage to get over but so far it was not showing much improvement except that he felt a little more energetic.

The first few days after massage and physiotherapy, he had terrible pain. Gradually over the week, he found the level of pain going down. Maybe his pain threshold had increased or maybe the pain was actually going down. He liked the young physiotherapist Matt who worked with him. The young man was full of energy and good to discuss politics and general topics with.

Scott told Matt that that he was quite surprised that he was so well read and could discuss world politics, business in general with such clarity. Matt told him that he actually wanted to be a news reporter but he also liked helping people. He decided to follow his passion to help people by working as a physiotherapist but sometime in the coming years, he would switch to journalism full time.

Neil was still coming almost every day and could see that Scott's spirits had lifted up a bit, but Sam and Ruby did not like this positive change in him and were scheming how to reverse the process and fast track their plan.

Neil came to discuss the project progress report with him but found Scott in deep discussion with Matt, so he too sat down. It was fun to see glimpses of the old Scott. However, Neil had also seen him on the other side of scale, totally frustrated and desperate, only a few days back. He wanted Scott to be happy and it pained him to see him go through such varied and extreme emotions.

After Matt took his leave, Scott asked Neil about how things were at work. Neil poured out about various issues they were having and asked Scott for his view to resolve the issues. Scott, who had always kept his company interest first, let go of what he wanted to say to Neil but helped him to formulate a plan to resuscitate the situation.

Neil thanked him and asked him about his progress with physiotherapy to which Scott just laughed and said,"You can see I am still in the same bed with same assistance required so let's not kid ourselves." Neil asked about Matt and Scott said that he was very intelligent and wanted to make a career in journalism. Scott was sure that he would be a good and passionate journalist not like the ones who could be easily swayed. Neil heard his pointed and caustic remark but did not want to get into that discussion. Somewhere deep down Neil knew he was responsible for it too and the barbed remark was for how he had managed the situation. Neil knew Scott was smart and it would not be long before he caught up with him. He tried to make light of situation and tried to cover up with trivial talk about different sites. He even tried to tell some stories from office.

It was getting late and as Neil was getting ready to leave, Ruby walked in. Scott waved her in and then thanked Neil for his help. Neil got the hint that he should leave. He walked out but Sam was making him slow down to hear what was being discussed. Ruby closed the door and Sam could see from her gestures that the argument was not going smooth, Scott was getting strained and both were talking in a heated manner. Sam walked out humming to himself.

Sam came to the parking lot and rather than going to his own car, leaned onto Ruby's car and waited for her to come out of the hospital. He really wanted to hear what happened before Ruby had any time to cook up a new story. He did not have to wait for very long. As expected, Ruby came out in about fifteen minutes and walked straight to her car. She did not notice Sam leaning against her car. She was a bit startled by his presence and looked around to see who all, if anyone, was there.

The parking lot was deserted with only a few cars parked and no-one was in the vicinity. She was seething with anger and to avoid shouting, clenched her teeth and snarled at Neil, "What the heck is wrong with you? Why couldn't you wait for a little longer to find out what was going on?"

Sam shamelessly said, "No, actually I cannot, and now that we have established at least this fact, why don't you go ahead and let me know what is going on?" She said, "If we are going to work together, we need to develop trust between us." Sam replied angrily, "Yeah and that is a two way street so why don't you start being upfront and tell me what's going on rather than using these delaying antics".

Ruby was a bit taken aback by this brazen attack but she kind of liked this new Neil. She said "Ok if you must know, let's at least sit inside the car rather than standing in the parking lot and discussing it. It makes me feel bit awkward." Sam gladly agreed with a devilish smile and like a true gentleman, asked her - "Yours or mine?"

She made a face at him and unlocked her car. Both got in and then she told him that she had been trying to plant the seed of a break-up in Scott's mind but she wanted it to be his idea. Today Scott again asked her to leave him alone and the argument only added another brick in the wall which was coming up fast between them.

Sam found it quite appealing and leaned over to kiss Ruby. Ruby turned her face away, Sam could not tell her that he was clearly having a difficult time controlling himself around her and every time he heard her speak he just wanted to hug her, kiss her and be with her forever. He said, "You seem to be the missing part of me." Ruby laughed aloud and told him teasingly to get out of her car.

Sam obliged but said half-jokingly, "One day you will pay for kicking me out of your car." Ruby only smiled and gestured for him to leave. Sam got out of the car but could not get Ruby out of his mind, and he was sure she had guessed how smitten he was by her.

Sam moved to his car but on second thoughts decided to pay a visit back to Scott and see what he could gather from him or maybe from his phone if he was lucky. Sam came up to see Scott watching television. He knocked and entered to see the attendant pestering, and pleading with Scott to have his night medicine.

He asked Scott if he could sit for a few minutes with him. Scott nodded. Sam gestured the attendant to leave them alone for a few minutes. Once the attendant left, Sam turned to Scott. "What is eating you Scott? I know something is bothering you." Scott poured out his heart, "I love Ruby a lot but I cannot let her spoil her life for me." Sam looked at him in disbelief and said - "Scott, you are going to be back on your feet in a few months and you two will have a wonderful life together." Scott said, "Dear friend, if you must know I do not think we will. I think Ruby is too smart and too out of league for a half-broken man like me. She needs to move on and

I have decided that I am going to tell her to not come here anymore and I will talk to my parents too about my decision".

Sam tried half-heartedly to dissuade him but he knew that Scott could not be swayed. Finally, he said, "If that is what you think is the best then I do not want to force you." Scott suddenly looked at him and said, "I know you care a lot for me but there is a complication."

Scott gestured Sam to move closer and then whispered, "Ruby is pregnant, she told me this today and I have decided to give her two million as a bank deposit and a house so that she can have a life of comfort. I do not want my child to be deprived of any comfort so I will also support her financially and this was the reason of our fight today."

Sam was actually shocked at the masterstroke the lady had played. She managed to get a great deal from this man who was blindly in love with her. Sam told him, "I think you should have your medicine and sleep, we can discuss this tomorrow, I will drop in before I go to office and meanwhile I am taking your phone which is nothing but a distraction for you." Despite loud protests from Scott, Sam picked up his phone and called out to the medical assistant to give Scott his medicine.

Sam left the hospital and drove straight to Ruby's house. He rang the bell impatiently and when she opened the door, he looked at her and all his resolve to fight with her dissolved. He asked her, "Are you really pregnant? " Ruby smiled and said, "I knew the curious in you would go and ask Scott and then come here to seek the truth." Sam was again surprised at how well she knew him. She said, "I might be but if I am not you are here to make it happen."

Sam slept at Ruby's place with her in his arms dreaming of a nice house and what all he could buy with that two million. In the morning, he was woken up early by Ruby to "get out" before the house cleaner or anyone else saw him. He kissed her goodbye and left.

Sam went home and after a quick shower copied all the files from Scott's phone and subsequently deleted the data. Then he dropped the phone and violently crushed it with his shoe repeatedly. Then he did a dress rehearsal - picked up the phone - and made a real sad face - "Scott, your phone ...I am really sorry is totally damaged, I dropped it while on the way here", then he laughed aloud and left for the real take at the hospital.

He reached the hospital in an extremely cheerful mood following the developments and events of last night. Sam went straight to Scott's room. Before entering, he changed his current state of mind to look gloomy and sad. He said - "Scott, I am really sorry. I was in a hurry this morning and I dropped your phone and damaged it completely, I will get you a new one from the company computer department in a day or two." He was even able to shed a tear thanks to the orange peel he had squeezed in his eye just before coming in.

Scott looked at the mess in Neil's hand and said, "Oh no! This mobile had all my data and work and I did not even back it up to the cloud yet." Neil apologized and asked Scott to give Neil a day or two and he would have a brand new phone. He would try and see if anything could be recovered from the phone.

Sam walked out patting his own back for his Oscar worthy performance. He walked to the car got in and drove to the office. He met Alex, the Vice President and appraised him that Scott was not feeling too well and that he was taking the recent setback not too well. He was very frustrated and had even smashed his phone. He showed the remains of the phone to him.

The Vice President nodded his head and said, "I am a little disappointed but we cannot keep this company at a standstill. I applaud your efforts to spend time in office and then with Scott to keep him company every day. You are truly a valuable asset and Scott did well to find you."

Sam was drip feeding the stories to the Vice President for a few weeks now and he was getting the impression that he had planted a tree of doubt about Scott's well-being in his head. He wanted to nurture it for some time before this tree bore the fruit, which he had waited for some time now.

He walked to his (Scott's) office and took out the file of fresh ideas, which he had saved from Scott's phone. Before starting work, he picked up the phone, dialed the computer department, and asked him to program the new phone for Scott by the next day. He also asked him to look if any data could be retrieved from the old phone. Computer department told him they did not have a phone available, he told that he will get one for them immediately as an emergency purchase.

Sam called one of his smart friends and asked him to buy a new phone and install a spyware whereby he would have remote access to all the files on this phone. He asked that this phone should be delivered to him by the end of that day. His friend tried to tell him that he had too much of work, but he cut him short and said, "I can pay you extra but I need the phone and the bill today."

Having resolved the phone issue much better than he expected, he sat back and extracted the information from his notes and put it in a Powerpoint presentation. He reviewed the budget figures to make sure all was okay, and then he called the contracting firm manager for the site which had the accident and asked him to meet him for lunch in the afternoon..

He walked out of the office and left for a quick tour of the site before meeting the contractor. He had a quick walk about and asked the new site manager who was an old friend about the work-situation. The person wanted to please Neil so he said that everything was fine.

Suddenly Sam got up from the chair, held the site manager by his collar and said – "I do not care about the site, or the work here; make sure you do the job for which I have employed you. From now on every bill should have five percent for me or else do not bring any invoice to me."

With another task resolved with the stamp of his authority, he left the site and went to have lunch. He met the contractor and appraised him of the latest arrangements. The contractor was working with the company for many years and refused to tow this line. Neil said, "Either you do as told or I will make sure you not only lose this job but also all other contracts with my company." He further added, "Do not forget that all the big companies work together so if you do not work with us, you will not work in the industry either." He went on, "I did not call you here to ask you. I am telling you how business will be done from now onwards. Please make sure your site representative is aware of this arrangement." The contractor looked at Neil, but saw Sam looking back at him with utter disregard and stone hard eyes which conveyed the message in no uncertain terms.

The contractor asked, "But how will I make this margin work?" Sam told him, "Be smart, be innovative, use whatever methods you want to employ as far as the houses do not collapse and no one dies on site. Also remember that I resolved your dead man issue else you would be pretty much still on media channels clarifying your work ethics. Think of this as a small payback for what I did for you."

Sam added, "This is a social project funded by the government, who only cares that we deliver, the people who will buy it only care that they get a house, no one is going to look at the fine print and I don't think I need to teach you how to use this to our advantage."

Finally they both shook hands and parted ways with an understanding that Neil gets his five percent but any future bids would feature the contractor firm as the preferred contractor. The contractor firm was a family business and all he had to do was to sell it to his brothers and father. He knew that his father might have some issues but he would need to play it in a certain way to ensure the business could prosper.

Sam thought that he had a very productive day and decided to celebrate a little. He called Sandra, who answered on the first ring and agreed to meet him at her apartment. Neil told her, "I will not stay long." Sandra said, "I hope you stay long enough for both of us to have some fun."

Sam decided to drop by and see if the phone was ready. He walked into Rahim's office located in his garage and shouted, "Hey Rahim, what about my phone?" Rahim came out and told him, "It will be ready in half an hour. It is being programmed." Scott told him that he would be back in about 45 minutes.

Sam went straight to Sandra's place and was happy to find her alone. He stayed there for about 30 minutes, and having satisfied himself, drove back to pick up the phone. He got Rahim to swipe his credit card for payment and took the new phone. Rahim put the bill in the phone box and handed over everything to him in a bag. He also handed over a sheet with codes and procedure how to retrieve the data remotely.

Rahim offered him tea but Sam declined saying that he was in a hurry and left. He went straight to office and climbed up to the computer department, handed over the phone to them and instructed them to format it as soon as possible. Before they could argue or say something, Sam said, "Scott really needs all the help we can give him, so please finish it. I will wait in my office and I will deliver it personally to Scott myself on my way home."

He thanked the computer technician and told him, "If you do this for me, I will owe you a cold one." The guy said, "One, nah a couple", both laughed and Sam said, "a whole case of cold ones, man".

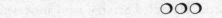

9

Neil looked at some emails and saw the progress report of different sites while Sam was waiting for the computer technician to complete the configuration. He wanted to check whether the spyware loaded by Rahim worked.

The Vice President passed by and asked him if all was ok. He said, "Yes, I am only reviewing the reports and waiting for Scott's new phone to be configured so that I can give it to him today itself. I don't want him to feel left out of the loop." The Vice President nodded, asked him not to work very late and have a little life of his own too.

The computer technician finally finished the configuration at 8 pm and came to deliver the phone as Sam was debating to leave without the phone. Neil invited him for a beer as promised. He wanted to show that he meant what he said. Sam as always felt that having the computer technician on your side can be beneficial. He picked up his coat and told the computer technician, "Let's go, I will drive."

Both left the office and went to a nearby bar where everyone knew Neil. The place was almost packed but they managed to arrange a table for him. That is one of the perks one gets if they are a regular and well known to a place. Sam ordered two beers and then once they got them, he made sure the computer technician's glass was full at all times. After a couple of beers, the person started talking and poured out all his past and present to Neil. Sam picked up some interesting information about his past about hacking and told him that maybe we can work together and receive mutual benefit.

Finally Sam left him still drinking with another couple of drinks on the way for him. He made sure that the guy was totally sloshed. On exiting, he told the bartender to make sure that his friend finished his drink. He also asked the bartender to book his friend a cab to go home. He gave a generous tip to the bartender, and an extra amount which would be enough to cover the taxi fare leaving few extra bucks as tip for the taxi driver.

Sam had not drank more than one beer but he still drove cautiously. Scott was quite surprised to receive a new phone this quickly. Sam then added that unfortunately the data could not be recovered from the old phone. He updated Scott regarding some information about the sites but not about his deal with the contractor or the site manager. When he was leaving the hospital, he realized he had forgotten to try the spyware and he was really annoyed with himself. He vowed to check it as soon as he got home.

He came back home to see the lights were on and when he entered, he saw Ruby there with dinner laid on the table. She smelled the beer in his breath and said angrily, "I was here making dinner for us to celebrate and you were partying with your other friends!" He explained to her about the accident with Scott's phone and how he had to wait for the new phone to be configured by his technician colleague before giving it to Scott. To show his gratitude to his colleague, he had taken him out for a drink. Ruby waved it aside and said, "You don't have to explain. We are not married yet. Go and change meanwhile I will get the food warmed up."

Sam was surprised with this avatar of Ruby but he played along. Sam showered, changed and came for dinner to find warm food on the table and a bottle of expensive red wine open and poured in glasses. He joked, "So the idea is to get me drunk?" She said, "Then what? I will get what I want anyway. You better not spoil my mood, let's have dinner and try to sleep early."

Once dinner was over, they went to bed. She slipped next to him and whispered to him, "I am pregnant and I want you to marry me, and believe me, the kid is yours." He did not know whether to cry or laugh but he said, "Yes, let's get married". She said, "Not now but after we have collected the promised bounty from Scott."

Sleep was miles away from either of them but while he was still blabbering about all the luxury he would shower upon her she started to snore lightly. Neil was wondering why she wanted to marry him and how would he explain to Scott. Sam had no such thoughts, he was dreaming about walking around with her hand-in-hand to the envy of other men.

Sam remembered that he had to try his spyware so he quietly tip-toed from the bedroom to his room. He opened his laptop and connected to the site. It worked like a dream. He could not only get all the phone call records, text messages, emails but also knew where Scott was. Not that Scott was going to move out any time soon. But he was mighty pleased with Rahim's work.

He would not have to sneak out the phone now, this only meant one less thing to worry about. He shut the system and went back to bed. He looked at Ruby sleeping in the bed looking so beautiful. He slid in quietly next to her, holding her tightly in his arms. She stirred and then settled into a comfortable position. He too went to sleep.

Next morning Neil got up to see Ruby had already left. He too got up, went to take a shower and got ready for office. He had planned to visit some other sites outside the town over the next few days. He also wanted to give Ruby some time to play her game.

He decided to talk to the Vice President about his overdue tours to other project sites and do it as soon as possible. He walked into his office, spoke to the Vice President about his plan who seemed pleased to hear about it, and nodded his consent.

Sam was happy that he did not have to push for it. Then he got down to preparing a list of all the contractors and site managers he would meet. He also wanted to collate all information of the other projects so that he could see which contractor had how big a share of the company business. Scott had all this information memorized but Sam needed to get it collated.

He called up the secretary and told her his plan to visit the sites over the next few weeks. Then he started contacting all the site managers and asked them to be ready for a site inspection and progress report on site.

The day passed very quickly with him being busy with all the schedules and information collation efforts. Finally, he left office but did not want Scott to know he was on to something. He went to the hospital, and saw Matt deep in conversation with Scott. He went in and asked, "How is Scott doing today?" Matt replied, " With all the effort and hard work being put in eventually we expect to get results."

"I would like to discuss a few things with you. Scott." Matt hurriedly got up and said, "I am done and was just keeping Scott company." Neil appraised Scott about his idea to visit a few sites. Scott said, "That is a good idea. It will also help to develop personal rapport with the site managers, which is very important."

Sam smiled and thought to himself, "Yes, I know but you do not know." Neil asked Scott for some guidance on a project where they were having a few challenges. Within minutes, Scott managed to come up with possible solutions and gave him an estimate of the cost involved.

Finally, Neil asked him about Ruby. Scott told him that she was not happy about his decision for her to move on with life. He requested Neil to arrange to move his things from his flat to his parent's place as he was planning to move there once he was discharged.

All this was news for Neil. "So what do we do about the house?" Scott told him to look for a place too as he was transferring the ownership of that house to Ruby which unfortunately meant Neil would have to move out. Neil tried to reason with Scott. He had already been successful in making Scott understand the other part of the story but this time it seemed he was not going to change his mind. Scott kept insisting that he had given it a very good thought, as time was the only luxury he had.

Neil told him Ruby would never agree to leave him, not in his current state. Scott just laughed and said, "It is not her decision, it is mine and the decision is already made."

Finally, with not much else to discuss, Neil bade him goodbye and left.

OOO

10

Sam first visited the site that had the maximum budget allocation. This site had a huge office and the contractor was the same with whom he had already made a deal. He knew this would be quite easy. What he did not know that the site manager was a classmate of Scott and was quite envious of his progress in the company. Scott had warned Sam against him on the last day before he left for inspection.

While discussing with him, he casually mentioned Scott and he could see his tone and attitude change immediately. Every time he mentioned Scott, he could see the reaction. Finally, when he was about to close the meeting, he mentioned to him, "You have an axe to grind with Scott and I have an agenda which I want to fulfill so if you can work with me and do as I say, I think we both can benefit from this situation."

Sam finally managed to leverage the sour relationship of the site manager and Scott to his advantage. He was feeling quite satisfied with the outcome. With every outcome in his favor, Sam was getting more and more confident that his plan would succeed.

He left the site and went to the other site. With each success he was getting more and more brazen in his approach. Sam was cunning from the start but now a new dimension-- greed-- had been added. Greed was driving Sam and Sam was driving Neil.

In the next few days, Neil visited about ten different sites and had meetings with their site managers. All the sites were running like a well-oiled machinery. Sam's intention was not to interfere in the work, however he wanted to put his stamp of authority and ensure his own interest was taken care of.

After about a month of travel Neil returned to find that Scott was soon going to be discharged from hospital. Scott's father had arranged for a full time attendant and a part-time physiotherapist to take care of his treatment from home. Neil was a little hurt that when he had talked to Scott while on the tour he had not mentioned it even once.

Sam tried to understand what had changed. He even scanned all Scott's emails and text messages he was getting in his computer but could not find anything. Sam was surprised how things had changed in one month. He had created a ledger in his private computer to monitor all sites and what his agreement was with the various contractors. Some contractors had been forthcoming to give him what he asked in the hope that this would get them future benefits. He had failed to come to reasonable terms with only one site. He was now planning how to get his trusted lieutenant in that site installed so that he could either get the contractor to follow his way of working or get him declared incompetent and get rid of him.

Scott meanwhile had told Ruby in no uncertain terms that he wanted her to move on. She tried to dissuade him but not with much conviction. They had drifted apart in the last few weeks. Sam could see that Scott was trying to show he was not smitten by her as before and was doing everything to push her away. Scott had even screamed and shouted at her in front of hospital staff. Ruby too was not someone who was going to take this rude behavior lying down. Matters had escalated and after a bit of drama both Scott and Ruby mutually agreed to move on rather than nurture ill feelings about each other.

Ruby got the house papers registered in her name, the promised two million dollars and was happy to move on. Scott wanted to concentrate on his recovery. Neil as always was stuck between his loyalty towards his friend and being in awe of the beautiful Ruby. One day when they were discussing work, he asked Scott, "Ruby is pregnant and leaving her like this is not good." Scott told him, "I know, but I have no choice. You can see she is not very patient and before she does something which we all will regret I want her to move on."

Neil looked at Scott and said, "If you have no objection, I have a solution. I am willing to marry her and support her. I am possibly the only person apart from you who understands her." Scott looked at him and then burst out laughing - "I hope you know what you are saying, she is a high maintenance girl and prone to tantrums. Neil you are from a small town and although you have seen a lot in the last few years I don't think you can bell that cat. Remember she is not a cat but a tigress."

Sam wanted to tell Scott that he knew how to tame tigresses very well but he said politely, "I am only suggesting a way out whereby all this stays within our house and no one is wiser in the outside world. Already the press and reporters have repeatedly used your accident and then other things. I feel we can contain this and do some damage control."

Scott finally consented reluctantly but cautioned him to be careful. Neil left Scott and drove straight to Ruby's house to break the news. He had not told her that he was going to ask Scott for marrying her as he had no idea how Ruby would react. He reached her place and rang the bell.

Ruby opened the door totally sloshed and smiled at him. Sam looked at her face in disbelief and said " What the hell! You are pregnant and drinking is dangerous. She only smirked and said, "Neil, we are not married yet and please do not pretend as though you care." For once Neil lost his cool and was about to hit her, but he controlled himself.

Sam was going wild and wanted to celebrate too. Grabbing a glass he poured himself a stiff drink. He felt there was no use at this time trying to tell her about his talk with Scott. After downing the first glass quickly he poured himself another one. Ruby regaining some composure asked him, "What are you doing in my house at this time?"

Neil said, "I wanted to give you a piece of good news. I spoke to Scott and he is okay for us to get married." Ruby reacted as though she had received an electric shock. "Excuse me, what did you just now say? You asked for Scott's permission to marry me? How pathetic, I am totally disgusted. You and me are adults and we can decide what we want to do. Why did you have to go and ask Scott? Is he your bloody father or your priest without whose blessing we cannot get married?" In a fit of rage, she picked up a bottle and threw it at Neil in disgust and anger. Sam managed to duck in time.

The bottle flew across the room, hitting the wall and shattered to pieces on hitting the ground. Sam screamed at Ruby, "Are you out of your mind or crazy"? She just snarled at him and looked around to find something else to throw at him. Neil ran for his life but unfortunately stepped on the shattered glass pieces lying on the floor and fell. He felt a million shards go through his body. He screamed in agony and tried to get up.

Somehow he pulled out his phone to dial the emergency number for the ambulance when Ruby snatched the phone from his hand and disconnected the phone. She lifted him up and led him by his hand to the bathroom. She made him sit on the toilet seat cover and then removed his clothes and slowly pulled out the shards one by one from his back and hands. Then she cleaned him up and applied some antiseptic. Finally she took him to bed and made love to him.

He was not sure if it was the pleasure or pain but it did feel a lot different. Ruby, once finished, patted his cheek and said "You got a lot to learn". She then left him in bed with a dazed look. She went and made a drink for Neil. "Drink this, you will feel better." She then cradled him in his arms. Both of them slept after that consumed by all the high action drama and sapped of all energy.

Next morning when Neil woke up he could still feel a shooting pain in his back and when he looked in the mirror he could see a few red spots on the bandages. Ruby came to the door, looked at his painful expression and said, "Don't be a wuss, you will be fine in a few days."

Sam was now more determined to tame this tigress and not to mention, a multi-million dollar house and 2 million in cash were the added attraction which sweetened the deal for him.

Neil, on his return, made a presentation to the management about his visits to various sites and some opportunities for expanding business. He also appraised them about further opportunities on these sites.

Sam now started to work in earnest to get more business for the company, which eventually meant that he would stand to gain more himself too. He made sure that he was involved in every step at all levels and got involved in all stages from the launching of the request for information (RFI) to sending the request for proposal (RFP), getting the bids, evaluating them and making sure that his favorite contractors got the contract.

Sam was quickly sinking in the quicksand of greed. He wanted to maximize his gains but so far he had managed to keep the management out of the picture completely. This was really a surprise as one would expect some whispers to filter through. Currently with the construction business not doing well, the senior management was satisfied that the company was able to get new clients. The management team liked the progress and the bottom line was that the company was able to support its business needs and make some profit too.

The business had grown quite a bit in the recession market and most of the senior management attributed it to Neil's hard work. He was seen as the golden boy who had the Midas touch. Wherever he went he returned with positive results.

Neil was soon appointed ad-hoc manager and he took his job quite seriously but Sam only cared about his personal gain and was always looking to leverage this position to maximize his gains. He kept on getting more business which made the company grow but at a cost for which someday someone would have to pay a heavy price. Some of the colleagues and senior managers were not pleased with the meteoritic rise of Neil.

Neil and Ruby finally decided to get married. Ruby wanted a full ceremony where she could flaunt to her friends and others the young, good looking and handsome Neil. Neil was a bit uncomfortable with this approach but he did not want to pick a fight with her again.

He left the decision to Ruby but told her that they should rather than spending all this money on grandeur, use it to buy a better house or have a luxurious holiday all by themselves. Ruby did not want to hear or do any such thing. She had made up her mind a long time ago that she was going to have a grand wedding.

She resumed her preparations from where she had left before Scott had the terrible accident.

Some of their friends were surprised and some even felt a bit odd about this change in equation. Scott was the fiancé and now he was not. A few of their friends joked behind their back but no one said anything to them on face.

Neil and Ruby had a dream wedding followed by a two-week long honeymoon in a beach resort where all Sam did was worry about his work and how much money he was losing while he was sitting there with her. She was busy having a great time and forcing Neil to be with her. She spent her time in beauty parlours and massages or sipping drinks.

Sam was now getting a bit impatient and wanted to return to work not because he loved his work but because he thought that he would lose control of the real situation. He did not trust anyone in office. Before his patience reached the tipping point, two weeks were over and they returned back. Sam immediately got busy with his work and tried to recover the lost ground. Ruby was busy with gloating over her marriage and her honeymoon to anyone who cared to listen. They did not visit Scott or even ask about his well-being from his family or common friends.

Sam was so immersed in his greed that he started coming late at night. The novelty of marriage and the honeymoon story were wearing off for both of them. Ruby was getting a bit impatient. They had been married for three months now and Ruby already suspected Neil was cheating on her and having an affair at either the office or somewhere else. She asked him directly a couple of times and it only irritated Sam. He too started losing patience with her and answered rudely.

Ruby was now almost in her second trimester and the weight of pregnancy and her suspicion of Neil was taking a toll on her. Invariably, they would start an argument with neither of them having the patience to listen and both would end up screaming at each other. Later, no one would have food and they would go to bed hungry. Normally, next morning usually Neil tried to make up with her because he could not bear the thought of her being hungry as it could affect the baby.

At times Ruby felt remorseful and they would kiss and make up and normalcy would return to the household but it never lasted for more than a few days.

The arguments would either be about Neil staying late at office or Ruby going out to meet her friends or going to work when Neil wanted her to stay and take rest. It seemed as though both of them were observing each other all the time and waiting to find an opportunity to pick an argument.

Sam felt that Ruby was being irrational and not understanding. He would make his displeasure known quite openly now and Ruby would not be far behind either. She would pick up the issue of her pregnancy and not looking as beautiful as she used to a few months back, a point she knew would infuriate Neil. It would appear that she drew some pleasure from Neil's pain.

Meanwhile time flew past unknown to either of them. Scott was doing quite well and after the last round of operation he was recovering at a good pace and was responding to physiotherapy too. He could not stand or walk but he was getting some sensation back in his limbs. He was putting in real hard work to get better. He pushed himself to the limit, so much so that the physiotherapist had to stop him lest he may cause more harm than good to himself.

Sam was getting impatient at home and quite dominating at times. Ruby did not spare any chance to remind him that he may be a senior manager in the office but at home, she was the one who would be in charge. The heavier she got with time, the more demanding she became. This could been acceptable were it related to her pregnancy only but she used her pregnancy as an excuse to leverage whatever she thought she wanted from Neil and from anyone else too. She made Neil buy a bigger mansion with the argument that the family was going to grow and they needed more space. They already had a four bedroom house which would have sufficed but she insisted that they buy a huge six bedroom duplex mansion and now she forever cribbed that she was restricted to the first floor as she could not keep going up and down. Sam thought of reminding her that this was not his choice and he had to arrange a huge mortgage to please her but that would have only added more fuel to the fire so he kept quiet.

Neil was burdened with a lot of work at office and did not want any more issues at home. Most of the time he tried to keep quiet and let it go but some days he lost his cool.

However unknown to him, this gave Ruby a sort of power over him. Every time he did not fight back, it made Ruby feel a little bit more stronger and she started to not only fight but insult and demean him. At times, she used to call him names and try to provoke him. She received pleasure from playing this game. She was now confined to the four walls of the house not because of any compulsion but of her own free will. This was because she wanted to get back in shape before socializing with her friends or going to parties.

Time was ticking and so was the "Ruby bomb". With each passing week, she was getting more and more impatient and unreasonable Neil had no idea how to deal with her, so he gave her free rein. Maybe that was a mistake? The trouble was that he had no way of knowing how to deal with her. If he tried to help her, she screamed at him and if he ignored her, hell broke lose. He was in a typical "no win" situation.

11

When they were buying this new house, Neil had asked Ruby to pool in some of the cash she had received from Scott. She kept giving him excuses for a while and later flatly refused. "You are the man and it is your duty to provide and not beg from me." Sam was furious that day but now he knew that he had to build his own kitty too.

He opened an offshore account without telling Ruby and started parking some money there. Today he was opening his third such account in a little known tax haven and away from the prying eyes of Ruby and others.

A few weeks passed in the baby shower preparation and then the actual event was held in a beautifully decorated home. Ruby was busy with all the preparation and looking beautiful. She was off Neil's back for a while which gave him some time to redefine his strategy. He consulted a financial consultant who gave him tips on how he could make his accounts invisible to his wife and how to invest it in different parts of the globe where little or no questions would be asked. There was some risk involved but Sam, whose entire life was like a big gamble, was not going to shy away from it.

Finally, the baby was born, and Neil thought that his misery would end. Little did he know that matters would get worse. Neil's misery increased manifold as he, despite trying to be home and being with the baby to take some load off Ruby, was still being blamed for her sleepless nights and day long struggles with a baby.

Neil had trouble understanding the illogical situation he was in. He employed a full-time nanny, stretching his known financial resources further but still nothing seemed to make Ruby happy. It was clear that she was ill prepared for life with a child. Neil loved being with the child although he could not understand why the baby had black curly hair.

Sometimes when he was alone, Neil used to doubt if the baby was really his. Neil thought of getting the DNA test done but knew this would raise another storm at home. When Neil saw the baby smile, the whole world seemed to stop and all his doubts and inhibitions were lost and forgotten. Once home from work, he used to be around the baby trying to soak in as much of his love as he could.

At work, things were progressing well. Sam managed to keep all his personal dealings below the radar and continued to gain and add to his kitty in offshore accounts. He wanted to have a few millions, which would give him the cushion when he would need it. He had already been made well aware that what Ruby had was not for him.

Neil was trying to make the marriage work and he had thought the baby would make things better but Ruby thought the baby had ruined her career and any chance she had of a career. Neil tried to reason with her, "See you have such a beautiful family !" But she would not listen to any of it and would always blame him and his selfish nature to have stifled her career even before it took off.

Now even Neil started to doubt whether he had a great life and a wonderful family. He too started to blame himself for the misery Ruby was in. Sam was the carefree one who understood Ruby's game. She was blaming Neil for a career she had never had and he would joke to himself that how could someone stifle her career when it never existed.

Sam was making himself indispensable at work. He had not only taken over the entire portfolio of Scott had but expanded it multifold. He knew exactly how to keep the senior management happy with news of future growth and delivering it. Every monthly meeting had his graphs going north even in an otherwise depressed market.

He was becoming the envy of other departments and senior managers. It was also the reason why most of the people kept quiet and continued to work with him. His growth and progress gave reason for other departments to stay afloat.

Once the finance manager attempted to start an enquiry into the financial dealing of a contractor which showed some irregularities. An internal inquiry was held and Neil was acquitted with no proof of corruption or wrong-doing. Sam went out of his way to ensure that the life of the finance manager was made unbearable. He hired some thugs, got the finance manager's car vandalized, his house ransacked, and his wife and kid subjected to fearsome experiences. All of which affected the whole family and finally the finance manager resigned and quit.

The modus operandi was simple: either you let Sam have his way or if you tried to interfere with him, you were forced to leave with conditions turning unpleasant and unbearable. No one had proof that this was being done by Neil but most of the other managers took this as a warning not to cross his path.

Sam had created a reign of terror in the company but was still not visible to the senior management. Recently Sam became a lot brazen in his efforts. He used force, lies and other influence to ensure people who could speak against him were silenced. Most of the employees either closed their eyes or looked the other way rather than confront him. His stature in the company was getting more invincible and far from the reach of mere mortals in the company.

Sam was doing extremely well in the office. He was hailed as the business talent of the year in the company and outside. At the home front, the little Alexandre was growing up too. He had started crawling and was quite a handful. He would laugh every time he saw Neil. Neil too would play with him and got some relief from an otherwise stressful life at work and home.

The dreams or memory flashes were not as frequent as they were in the past. Neil occasionally saw himself all alone in strange and unknown places, living a nomadic life. His flashes were always short and before he could get enough details, either the dream would end or he would wake up. Neil had tried to close his eyes and go back to sleep so that he could complete the dream. No matter how hard he tried, it remained hazy incomplete sketches.

Ruby blamed him for messing up her future and body, and getting very caustic in her comments but Neil wanted to keep things under control so that Alexandre did not get affected. This would mean Neil had to ignore some of the caustic comments of Ruby, or try not to respond as he has learnt the hard way that this would make matters only worse.

Sometimes Neil remembered what Scott had told him once - be careful of Ruby, she can be a difficult person in the best of times. Now it seemed to Neil that his past was coming to bite him in his ass. Neil missed his daily bouncing of ideas off Scott. He did call up Scott occasionally, if not once every week, and visited him whenever he could.

Scott was living in his parents' house and with the mutual "love" of Scott's mom towards Ruby known to all, the best course of action was that Neil visited Scott as and when he could most of the times without telling Ruby.

Neil always found that Scott had a sobering and calming effect on his frayed nerves. He also felt guilty how Sam had managed to pull Ruby away from Scott. Neil thought that he could have changed the course of his life and that of everyone involved but he also knew Sam a little bit and how Sam controlled things and situations. He had no chance to wrestle control back from Sam.

Neil decided to visit Scott before coming to office and talk to him about the various issues at home with Ruby and little Alexandre. He was going to leave early today and swing by Scott's parents' house. Lately he had been working late hours and he knew that if he was a little late no one in the office was going to question it and everybody would assume that he was at a site or in a meeting with a prospective client.

Neil left home early despite protests from Ruby, which he had started ignoring lately. He reached Scott's parents' house quite quickly due to little traffic because he was going in the opposite direction to traffic flow.

He found Scott awake and in good spirits today after he had gotten rid of his wild facial hair growth of a few months. Neil asked Scott what the occasion was for this change of look. Scott looked up, smiled and lifted his right hand a little.

Neil was surprised and genuinely happy for Scott. He could not bear the thought of his friend-mentor being in bed for the rest of his life.

Neil responded that this wonderful news called for a celebration. He ran to get two glasses and a bottle of diet coke. He told Scott that this was going to be their intoxicant for the day. Both of them took a sip and Scott smiled after a long time. Scott told him that his left hand needed help but his right arm was working, although after a while he felt tired. Neil did not say anything but looked at Scott's legs. Scott followed his gaze and said - "I do believe that these legs too will move soon. I can feel some sensation in them with acupuncture."

Neil did not want to spoil what was such a happy day for Scott, so he just chatted about normal things and little bit of work, bounced off some ideas, picked his brain and then left after apologizing for his infrequent visits in the last few weeks. Scott smiled and told him he understood that his family and social burdens were bound to take a toll on him.

Scott did not ask anything about Ruby or Alexandre, and neither did Neil offer any information. Soon Neil smiled and bade him bye and left for his office.

OOO

12

After a gruelling day at work, Neil was looking forward to a peaceful evening at home. But an eerie silence greeted him in the house. Neil announced his arrival "Honey, I am home", but heard no response. He climbed the stairs to his bedroom to find it in total disarray with smashed glasses and everything strewn on the floor and the bed, the bathroom door was ajar and things lying on the floor there too. The dressing room cabinets were open and most of Ruby's wardrobe either was on the floor or pulled off the hangers. He shouted "Ruby" again but got no reply.

Now he was really worried. His dream of having a quiet evening quickly dissipated and he fell in a shock. He knew what Ruby was capable of, and he was now hoping that this was a moment of insanity but looking at things he realized, this would have to be a grand moment of sanity. Neil pulled out his phone from his pocket and dialed Ruby's number. It kept on ringing. Neil then dialed the nanny's number who answered it on the second ring. When Neil asked her where was Alexandre, the puzzled nanny could only muster - "Sir?", Neil repeated his question, this time a little more slowly. She told him that Alexandre was with her in the park. She had picked up Alexandre and left when she saw Ruby throwing things and creating a havoc.

Neil asked her, "Did anyone come or call?" The nanny replied, "Yes Mr. Scott had called and when he asked, I told him about Alexandre. He asked to speak to Ma'am but she refused and then the long haired photographer came but he left soon after."

Neil thanked her and cut the conversation short telling her that he guessed where Ruby was. He called the French photographer but phone kept ringing. He tried Ruby's phone again but no response. In the next minute, he got a call from the photographer. Sam asked him angrily, "What's going on and where's Ruby?" The photographer told him that he had offered Ruby a shot back at modeling for which she was quite excited and was going to meet him in two hours. The photographer waited for four hours and finally canceled the shoot as she never turned up or answered any of his calls.

Neil talked for a minute or two just to be courteous but soon disconnected. Sam was furious and seething with anger. He heard a car stop in the driveway. He looked out from the window to see Ruby lurching back into the house.

Ruby seemed surprised to see him home so early. Sam was seething with anger and half-dragged, half-carried Ruby to the master bedroom. He dropped her on the bed and asked her to explain.

Ruby burst into tears and began to say something incoherently. After Neil managed to calm her down a bit, Ruby told him what happened.

Apparently the photographer had come with an offer for modelling and had fixed up a meeting with a client. She was quite excited and wanted to get ready for the meeting. When she tried on dress after dress, to her dismay, nothing seemed to fit her. She was really looking forward to going back to work and this assignment would have been a jump-start for her career. In frustration, she started to pull out things and then when nothing seemed to fit her, she threw things around, screamed and yelled. Neil could imagine Ruby being out of control and he knew how much pride she took in her looks.

A part of him felt sorry for her but then he remembered how this would have affected little Alexandre if the nanny had not taken him to the park.

He asked her, "So what is your plan?" She said that she had a long thought and she would like to begin some fitness and dance classes with a personal trainer to get back in shape. She would also arrange for some massage sessions with a personal masseuse to further quicken her getting back in shape. Neil could only think of what it would cost him.

He told Ruby that at present they could ill afford all these luxuries but she became wild. He tried to calm her down but to no avail. She finally taunted him about money and then Sam lost his composure, he hit her. He immediately realized this was not a wise move but in his anger he had lost his cool. He kept apologizing but Ruby kept humiliating him and when this was not enough, she scratched his face, neck and shoulders. Neil kept quiet and bore all the humiliation. He did feel guilty for hitting her but then two wrongs do not make a right. What he had done was not right but what she did could not be justified either. He kept blaming himself and put an ice-cold towel on her cheek while she kept hurling more abuses at him.

Finally, little Alexandre and nanny returned from the park and life in the household returned to somewhat normal. The time bomb, which was going to explode, seemed to have diffused. Little Alexandre came and hugged Neil and climbed to Ruby's lap. His touch seemed to calm her down.

To Sam, this was quite strange. This same Alexandre was being blamed for the situation by Ruby only a few minutes back. Sam tried to tell himself to stop trying to understand Ruby and concentrate on getting his own stash large enough so that he could escape. Neil was shocked to know what Sam thought or wanted to do. He wanted to stop him but had little say when it came to Sam.

Neil thought what would happen if Scott spoke to Ruby and told her about his recent success after months of working so hard. Neil realized that he had not told Ruby about Scott's condition or even about his visits to him but considering all what he had heard these last few hours, he thought it was better that he kept this information to himself for now. It would only add more fuel to the fire. He did not want this to be another cause of disharmony for days to come.

Alexandre stirred and said he was hungry. Neil quickly got up, took him from Ruby. "I will take him downstairs and feed him, bathe him and put him to bed." Ruby only smirked and taunted, "Wish you had ever said or taken such care of me." Once again, Neil ignored the pointed remark and left the room with Alexandre.

He came back after a couple of hours to find Ruby asleep on the easy chair. He took a blanket and covered her up. Ruby grabbed his hand and with eyes still closed said, "I am sorry for what I did to you. I should not have said all that I said and these scratch marks will look even worse tomorrow." Neil felt his heart skip a beat; he sat down next to her and apologized for hitting her. Neil then lifted her up and laid her on the bed. Neil asked her if she would like to have supper now or in a while. Ruby patted the bed next to her and told Neil to lie next to her for a while. Sam wanted to say no, but Neil could never do that to Ruby. He quietly laid next to her and kept his hand on her elbow. Ruby shifted his hand from her elbow to her torso and snuggled with him. She looked so innocent and child-like that Neil felt more remorse for hitting her.

Both slept without having any dinner and Neil even in his full suit with shoes on, managed to get some sleep. He did not want to move lest he disturbed her and soon he too dozed off. Neil got up at 3 am with hunger pangs and shoulder cramps to find Ruby rolling a cigarette. She had not smoked for at least a year now. He asked her if she wanted something to eat. She said, "I am fat enough and do not need to be reminded of it."

Neil went to the dresser, took a pair of boxers, changed into a t-shirt, and went down to grab something to eat. Afterwards he thought of making a sandwich for Ruby but then remembered her sarcastic comment. But Neil being Neil could not let it go. He made a small sandwich, poured a glass of fresh orange juice and took it upstairs to the bedroom. He left it on the side table with a little bit of noise so that she would notice it and then went back to bed.

13

Next morning, Neil got up with a bit of tingling in his face. He went to the bathroom to see angry welt marks on his body and face. He could not go to work like that. He called his office and reported sick. He next called his general physician and booked an appointment to see him. He could not afford to be away from work for too long.

Ruby woke up next morning as though nothing had happened. She wished him a cheery good morning, completely ignoring the welt marks on his face. Neil noticed that the sandwich he had prepared had been polished off. He did not say anything and left to join Alexandre in the nursery.

Alexandre who was not used to seeing him around was very happy to see him after the extended time they had spent together yesterday. They both got busy playing and soon forgot how much time had passed. The nanny came in and informed Neil that Ruby had left and had told her that she would not be home for lunch. When she went to pick up Alexandre for bath he refused. She was very surprised. Alexandre loved water and playing in his tub. Normally, Alexandre had to literally be dragged out of his tub.

Neil persuaded Alexandre to go for his bath and told him that he would continue playing with him after his bath. Alexandre, who was afraid that his dad would leave him if he went for a bath, he made Neil promise that he will not go away. Then only Alexander consented to go.

Neil used this time to check his emails and prepare some transfers and investments to his offshore account. Once finished, he made a few phone calls to check some work on a couple of sites. He suddenly felt a bit left out. Ruby had gone off somewhere unknown to him, Alexandre was busy with his little pleasures in the bath and Neil was in the house because he could not even go out to work due to his face being such a mess.

Sam picked up his mobile phone and called up the gym where he thought Ruby had gone and asked for her. He was told that she was there and, in a class, and unless it was really urgent, they would like to request him to call after the class was over. Sam was furious but he knew he could not do much since she held the key to the big pot of gold they had. He corrected himself -- the pot of gold Ruby had. He would never be invited to share any of her spoils.

Alexandre was back after his bath and demanded to sit on his lap. He picked him up and put him in his lap. He started talking to him but in a few minutes, Alexandre was softly snoring. All the effort of playing in the morning and then playing in the bath must have made him tired. Neil picked Alexandre up and took him to his bed. The nanny informed him that now Alexandre would only wake up for lunch.

Neil had a few hours to himself so he re-ran the drama in his head again. The drama he had witnessed yesterday, and it only made him more uncomfortable. He considered Ruby's reaction a bit over the top. He could understand her frustration but throwing around things and breaking things with a little child in the home was taking it a bit too far.

He had been observing Ruby closely for some time now and he realised that she was mentally unstable and it was dangerous to leave Alexandre alone with her. He did not want to advise her to seek counseling but he wished he could. Ruby definitely needed professional help.

He thought of asking a friend to help but he could not think of anybody reliable enough. It all depended on how soon something else came up, else he would be the toast and roast till then.

He decided he would let it pass and hoping with all this renewed effort on fitness she will soon get back her swelte figure and things would improve.

While he was deep in his thoughts, Ruby entered and asked Neil what was the matter. She told him that he looked as if he had seen a ghost. Neil made light of the situation and said, "I am the ghost right now." Ruby realized that this was a taunt for the face scratchings but chose to ignore it. She turned and walked into the bedroom informing him that her class had been great and now she was a bit tired. Ruby demanded Neil to draw her a bath and walked out expecting him to follow her.

Neil had no choice but to comply. He got up and followed her highness. He ran a bath with soothing salts and while she got ready for a dip. Finally she asked him, "I hope it does not hurt too much, but you got what you deserved so never ever raise your hand on me again." Neil apologized for the umpteenth time and told her that he was extremely sorry. However Ruby ignored his pleading apology, passed him the bath sponge, and got into the water.

Neil silently said to himself, "Your wish is my command master (then he corrected himself silently - your highness)" and got on with giving her back a scrub. Once or twice, when his hand came close to passing over to the front she quickly moved and gave him a piercing look and reminded him, "Mister, do not get any ideas after your recent act of brutality and hitting me. You are banished from coming close to me for a long time and don't you try to go looking elsewhere. I am going to watch you like a hawk. If I hear or feel anything is wrong, you would not have any balls left. I will make sure your balls are smashed and you can no longer be the playboy you think you are."

With this cold war on now, Sam was already plotting what he had to do to get some action. He did not care about her threats. He had fooled her in the past and would fool her again. If she could keep a hawk's eye on him he could be a slippery fish and just slip away even for a quick piece of action without her knowing during the day. Nowadays with site visits and contractor meetings, he could always create some time for his own pleasure.

14

A few weeks passed without any further drama and life was returning to some normalcy, if one could call it that. Neil was still a bit worried about Ruby and her refusal to talk to him.

One evening Neil returned from office to find Ruby sitting with a bottle of champagne. When he asked her what the occasion was, she told him she had managed to reduce 4 kg and was on track to fit into her pre-pregnancy outfits within the next 3-4 weeks. Neil was truly happy for her and he offered to have a glass to toast her success and hard work.

Ruby taunted him with his refusal to pay for the personal trainer and how she had to shell out money from her ever decreasing pot of gold, which she was saving for a rainy day. Neil acted as if he did not hear. He got a glass and joined her for a drink.

Ruby had almost finished three-fourth of the bottle all by herself, He poured half a glass, raised the glass as a gesture of toast to her and had a few sips. By then Ruby had already finished her glass and he poured some more into her glass. She said today she felt so happy that nothing could spoil her day.

They both soon finished their glasses and then went on to the second bottle of champagne. Soon Ruby was drunk and unsteady. Neil too was feeling a bit light on his feet. Both decided to finish their drinks in the bedroom. Ruby and Neil went to the bedroom hand in hand singing loudly.

Once in the bedroom, Ruby closed the door, got out of her dress and sat semi naked. Sam felt something stirring within him. He tried to get close to her and for once Ruby did not push him away. One thing led to another and they ended up making love and then in a drunken stupor went off to sleep.

Next morning the first thing Neil heard was a remark which cut him like a hot knife through butter. Ruby as soon as she was awake blamed him for taking advantage of her drunken state. Sam was furious and just threw the cup and saucer he had in his hand which crashed and shattered on the floor and stomped out of the room.

Sam was furious how this woman could be so self-centered. All she could think of was herself. Granted he should not have tried to make out knowing fully well Ruby would blame him afterwards, but at that time Sam was being driven by his other brain. Sam had to give full marks to Ruby -- she too had enjoyed, had her fun and now she had the gall to blame him for taking advantage of her. She really played this game well, she knew exactly what would work when.

Sam was amazed at the capability of this woman to wrap him around her little finger and make him do things against his will. He did not know why and how he lost control not once but so many times in the past. He never seemed to learn and every time fell for her cheap tricks.

Ruby is pregnant again, this cannot be true. Neil was having trouble grasping this reality. Ruby complained to him a few days back that her period was delayed but he told her to wait for a few days and it was over three weeks overdue when they went to the doctor. The inevitable happened.

Ruby abhorred the words 'rest' and 'take care of yourself'. She had just started getting back into shape and now she was pregnant. Ruby decided to go for an abortion but Neil would not hear of it. He literally begged her to not take such a cruel decision as it was only a matter of a few months and would not end her career.

For Ruby this was the end of her career. Another kid would be the burden she did not want, but every time the topic came up Neil gave her a few more compelling reasons why abortion was not a good idea.

Ruby too agreed with some of Neil's arguments that little Alexandre would have some company, and also that now since she is on a sabbatical another few months would not matter. Neil also promised to take good good care of her and family. She showed as if she was doing a huge favor to Neil.

Neil was delighted that he had managed to convince Ruby to keep the baby. He felt with another baby maybe Ruby and her mood swings might get tempered. At the same time having endured her tantrums during the first pregnancy he dreaded going through the same again. Neil did hope second time round would be little different and easier on him. Neil had no idea that Ruby had agreed to ensure she had another reason to blame him. Ruby would not let any chance to utilize her leverage to maximize her own comfort go away. She would make whimsical demands and poor Neil would comply to only keep peace. Soon once again the whole cycle of pregnancy, mood swings, body changes and Ruby cribbing about everything started.

Then started the get together for baby shower and arrival of the baby followed by a few days of frenzy when even Neil lost himself in all the happiness. They had a beautiful girl and they named her Laure, after Ruby's grandmother.

Normally with a new addition, the first child feels a bit neglected but here Alexandre was like a hawk and very possessive of his little sister. Alexandre did not like any stranger coming and picking her up or even getting close to her. He took his role of being the elder brother very seriously. He seemed to have matured beyond his age.

From the outside it looked like an ideal family with Neil having a stable job, a beautiful house, an attractive wife and two lovely kids. What else could a person ask for? But only Sam knew how difficult it was to juggle all the balls that he had to juggle. His children, a demanding wife and an ever increasing list of occasional flings.

Neil was on a high without any drugs so far but lately his new friend had got him introduced to recreational drugs. Neil liked being not in control and letting it all disappear in thin air even though eventually he had to be sober down before returning home.

Ruby soon suspected that something was not right. She started observing Neil very closely, Sam was a smart guy and believed he was able to fool Ruby with his excuse of extra work pressure and other such flimsy excuses. Ruby finally caught him red handed one day swallowing some pills. She questioned him what the pills were and why he was in such good mood after having them. He said these were placebos and they made him happy.

Ruby managed to sneak a few of his pills from the box to consult her friends. She soon realized that Neil was in deep trouble. He was not only fooling around with her friends but with other girls too. Neil was also into enjoying recreational drugs. She could not believe Neil would be so stupid as to fall for the drugs. She always believed drugs were for weak persons.

She confronted him but Sam fed her a made up story and refused to admit that he had a problem. Once again in her life Ruby was struggling to find a fix for her problems though it wasn't her problem but, since Neil was her husband so directly or indirectly it was her problem too.

She did manage to book an appointment with a doctor who agreed to be discreet and promised to clean up Neil's act sooner rather than later. The only hitch was Neil did not believe he had a problem. Ruby tricked him to take her to a clinic and he was now forced to face the doctor.

The doctor asked Ruby to leave them alone for some time. He spoke to Neil and told his own story how his dad was a drug addict and street dealer but his mom had the courage to kick him out and raise her three children all by herself but would not allow her kids to be exposed to daily issues of a drug dealer.

Neil did not offer any information about how he got involved in it and why he had started taking drugs. He agreed to the treatment. Ruby was pleased with the outcome and hummed in the car while on way back to the house.

Neil dropped her at the house and then went out without waiting for her questions or giving her any explanation. For the first time he felt the need to sit somewhere alone and think about his future. What the doctor had told him had really touched his heart and he wanted to come clean.

The next few months Neil worked hard with the doctor he not only gave up drugs but also became a devoted husband and father. It was a miracle that office and site work ticked along like clock work so he was able to keep his job.

Ruby too had toned down a bit. Possibly with two children to take care of it did not leave her with much energy to argue and fight. She was still nursing the ambition to rekindle her career soon. She began working out again to get back in shape.

She was always a very conscious and fit person who loved to exercise and look good so it was difficult for her to accept her current status. She asked Neil to participate with her in the fitness routine. Neil did not feel much need to exercise but agreed to work out with her at least twice a week. He thought this would gave them a little bit of time together and rediscover their lost relationship.

What Neil did not tell anyone was that it also helped him to fall asleep, he was again seeing things in his dreams. Every time in the past he saw something in his dream; the incident happened to someone close to him. Neil was a bit worried when in recent dreams he saw police cars, high prison walls and people in orange prison uniforms but usually either the dream went blank, remained hazy or he did not remember and got up with the noise from the dream only to realize he was in his own house in his own bed.

OOO

15

Neil could clean up his act but Sam would never leave him in peace. Sam always found a way to work himself back into Neil's life and meddle in his affairs. When Neil thought he was moving in the right direction Sam would raise his head and pull him in a different direction.

Neil thought being with Ruby he would be able to win back some lost ground in their relationship but Sam had other plans. He started to push Ruby too hard in the gym which only started to frustrate Ruby. Ruby loved working out but she was getting an impression that Neil had a strange notion, which seemed to be to show that how superior he was in the gym if not anywhere else. Little did Ruby know Neil had no control over Sam and it was Sam who was doing this.

One day while in the gym after having finished the regular one hour of training, Sam said he was tired and would like to take a break. Ruby told him to go ahead and she would join him in few minutes. Neil had a glass of water and then came back. Sam started pushing Ruby to go faster on the bike, he got on the bike and started pedalling hard and kept asking her too to go faster.

Ruby realized it was a mistake to ask Neil to join her in the gym, she was getting a bit overwhelmed with all this extra pressure. Ruby did gym not only to stay in shape but it gave her time to be with herself. Lately though she was being pushed to limits beyond what she enjoyed she was not liking it anymore.

Ruby was looking forward to getting back to her professional career and wanted to start working so that she could be independent. She wanted to establish herself again as a model and move on.

Ruby had great plans for her future but first the breakup with Scott and then two back to back pregnancies had taken some wind out of her sail. She still was quite attractive and had strong belief in her ability and willingness to put in the hard work so that she would succeed.

Typically female models have a limited time to leverage maximum benefit; especially after marriage and kids no one really wants to work with them in the fashion industry but it seemed people were still looking forward to work with her. Ruby was going to use all the attention she could get to bring her career back on track.

She kept in touch with her friends in the industry although Ruby was not naive and knew this was a dog eat dog field. No one was a real friend and everyone was a competitor, but she had her own fan following. The photographer friend whose work was well received by the fashion industry and he had connections, which would be extremely useful in her attempt to climb back into the rat race.

Ruby called another friend and photography genius for drinks and dinner one day. When she told Neil, Sam blew his top off and started screaming with his barbed remarks about always looking at excuses to invite people, her being a narcissist and only thinking about herself all the time, this venting went on for a few minutes. Sam realized quite quickly that he was not going to win this one so he too left it. Neil told Ruby he was sorry for his sudden outburst and he would support her in her career.

Ruby for once kept her cool and stayed composed. She wanted him to boil over and then said if you want you can go to your club and drink silly. I need help from him to get my career on track so I have invited him.

Neil played a perfect host on the day of drinks and dinner. He came home early showered and changed. He also helped to get the children showered and after their dinner put them to bed. He then opened a bottle of wine and offered a glass to Ruby.

Both of them were aware how their last binge drinking had ended up and did not want to be on same path again. After a few sips while they were still getting the dinner ready together the bell rang. Partosh came with a beautiful girl, Sam found it difficult to control himself and Ruby was already a bit put off that Partosh had company and Ruby would not be able to talk freely. Partosh greeted them and apologized for coming with a sudden and unannounced guest. He explained she was family and had come over for a few days. She had no plans for the evening and Partosh knew Ruby would not mind having an additional guest.

Neil asked both Partosh and his beautiful companion if they would like a glass of wine. Partosh said- "Of course I would not miss a chance to raid Neil's wine cellar." He told his companion Misha, "Ruby and Neil have a great wine collection and she must not refuse the great wine."

Misha said she had not seen a wine cellar before and Neil offered to show her theirs in a while. Everyone laughed and the tension in the air seemed to disappear. They all had a glass of wine and Partosh offered a toast to Ruby- "May you be back with a bang and rise to the dizzy heights you always wanted". Everyone chorused "Amen" and had a sip.

The talk was informal about Partosh's work, he also showed them pictures of Alexandre and Laure he had clicked which they all found quite cute and depicting the innocence of the children perfectly. Ruby asked Misha what brought her to town. Misha said she had never been out of her home town and after graduation wanted to see little bit of the world so Partosh had invited her to come over. Ruby chimed with some jealousy, "You are so gorgeous I am surprised Partosh has not yet cast you as a model in an advertisement yet."

Misha smiled and said, "I am not comfortable in front of the camera and Partosh knows it well and this is the reason he has never asked me to model for him." Sensing some tension building up, Misha told Ruby she had heard about her from Partosh quite a few times. She also added that she has heard Ruby's name being discussed by Partosh a few times already with some project directors. From what all she had heard she had thought Ruby would be a socialite but to be honest she found Ruby to be a great company and was simply awed by her elegance and poise. Ruby smiled and said, "You are very generous with your praise."

Sam was itching to be alone with Misha. He was totally smitten by her and could not contain his joy when Misha looked at him and asked "So do we get to visit the cellar?" Sam had to act up a bit- He said "Ruby and Partosh have some business to discuss and once they start that we can use the time to visit the cellar".

Soon Ruby and Partosh started discussing their work and Sam seized the opportunity to offer a tour of the wine cellar to Misha. Ruby just waved them off and continued her discussion with Partosh. Sam took Misha down to the cellar and bragged about the different wines there and how important it is to maintain the cellar atmosphere to ensure the wine stays in optimum condition. Misha expressed her ignorance with the finer points of wine.

Sam took the opportunity to explain to her the general misconception people have of older wines always being better which was not strictly true, it depends the year, quality of crop that year, from which region and then how it is bottled and stored. He said typically french wines are good as a rule of thumb, however now a lot of other regions of world do make some spectacular wines. Sam continued, another perception is if wine is bottled in château then it is usually better than the commercially produced and bottled wines. He also explained to her about sulphides in the wine and how they change the wine. Sam was obviously trying to impress Misha and keep her in the cellar as long as possible so that he could be close to her.

Sam was no wine connoisseur but with Misha having no knowledge about wines, Sam blabbered a few French words to give an impression that he knew a lot about wines. He was not even a wine believer, for him drink was something much stronger than wine. He always thought wine was to impress people and this was the reason he had bought all these expensive wines and built a cellar. Misha seemed clearly impressed with Neil's knowledge of a subject she knew little about and did not suspect that he was as ignorant about wines as she was.

Sam showed her some of the expensive wine he had in the cellar and impressed her by dusting the bottles and showing her the labels and giving off random prices in hundreds of dollars knowing fully well that Misha would not know the difference.

Sam offered to show her some more real cool places for wine if Misha so wanted the next day. They exchanged their phone numbers. In his head Sam was already planning how he was going to impress this girl. Misha was totally in awe of him by now and did not notice till Sam creeped up his hand to her waist and was holding her while talking to her.

Neil and Misha finally had to leave the cellar when Ruby shouted from top of the stairs that dinner was going to be served. Misha was a bit red faced when they came up from the cellar, while leaving the cellar Neil had brushed past her and she felt an electric current run through her body, her cheeks were a little flushed and she had goosebumps.

Sam noticed it all and knew when they meet next time he can make his move. As they came up Partosh asked Misha if she liked the tour and Ruby added, "I hope Neil behaved himself", and everyone laughed.

Dinner was expansive as always with Ruby going all out to ensure Partosh felt special. Ruby needed his help to revive her career and she was not leaving any stone unturned. She had prepared the fish which Partosh loved among other delicacies and also had got some Indian sweets to ensure Partosh sweet tooth was well taken care of too.

Partosh, Neil and Misha enjoyed the lavish dinner while Ruby nibbled on her green salad and boiled chicken diet.

Misha looked at her salad and said "This is another reason why I do not wish to be a model, see the sacrifice you have to make, leaving all this excellent food and living on salads and lean meat."

Ruby forced a smile and said, "Yeah, and still no one understands this hard work and sacrifice not even my own friends", Ruby winked at Partosh and said, "Hope you are listening?" Partosh who was happily tucking away the fish looked up and said, "Don't you worry, you will shine in our next shoot. Just keep up with the diet and keep glowing."

After dinner they moved to the lounge and had some chocolate and coffee, and finally Partosh and Misha bade goodbye after thanking Neil and Ruby for an excellent evening and wishing Ruby a new and impressive start in her second attempt.

16

Ruby again got busy with her fitness regime and was happy that Neil had decided to drop out from the gym routine and leave her in peace. Ruby was not aware that Sam had left her alone only to have more time with Misha. While Ruby was busy getting back to her career, Sam was meeting Misha and showing her around. His current focus was to find any excuse to be closer to Misha. He was driven by a desire to which he could not say No…It had been a while since Sam has pursued someone with so much dedication.

He took her to a wine tasting event and to see a cellar at a friend's place. Misha was amazed by the friends Neil had and his influential status. Sam took her to boutique shops and places to eat which she had only seen in movies..!! She was totally smitten by all this attention.

Sam was taking it a bit easy and from the first time he had put his hand around her waist to holding her hand lightly and guiding her or assisting her to get down from the car all was part of his act and came naturally to him. He kept showering her with lavish gifts and introducing her to a life of comfort. He could sense that Misha was indebted to him and then he played his final card.

He took her for a lavish lunch, ensured she had a little liberal dose of Aperitif, wine with lunch, and followed by a glass of port wine to end the lunch. Sam could see that Misha was a bit drunk and her speech was getting slurred. Now was the time for the final act. He guided her to a room in the hotel which he had pre-booked anticipating how the lunch would progress. Sam asked her if she would like to have some coffee. He made a coffee but Misha never got to drink it. They were soon in bed assisted by all the drinks they had had.

Misha was still sleeping and Sam was preparing for the outburst she would have when she woke up. He had prepared a speech and rehearsed it a few times already. He could feel Misha stirring and he got up to get a coffee for her now. Misha got up holding her head in her hand and complained about a heavy head and a bit too much to drink. Sam offered her the coffee and then slowly it dawned on Misha were she was. She freaked out and started to cry. Sam although prepared for this was not ready for the crying and had a little trouble getting started with his rehearsed act.

Once he started then it was all a performance worthy of an Oscar. He blamed himself for everything for the drinks and how both of them were a little intoxicated and how his life was a troubled one. Ruby was not the woman she seemed, how Ruby ruled over him and abused him, which was not all false although a bit exaggerated. Sam even managed to shed a few tears and suddenly both Misha and Sam were trying to console each other.

Finally Sam requested Misha to please not let this one act spoil their friendship, how sorry he was, and how he got weak for a few moments. Misha did not say anything but Sam made her promise that she will not speak to Partosh or Ruby about it else Neil's life would be a living hell.

Once Misha agreed to keep it a secret, Sam heaved a sigh of relief. He kept apologizing on the way down to the lobby and then while driving her home. Neil went back to office and Sam was full of energy revitalized by his recent performance.

Sam felt like a man who had won a million dollars. He kept playing the afternoon in his head and was wondering if he would be able to take Misha out again.

Sam thought he would give it a few days and then test the waters again. He did not have to wait long. Misha called him next day crying and complaining that she was thinking about their last afternoon together and feeling guilty. Sam calmed her down and asked her to meet him for coffee at a popular cafe downtown so that they were around people and they were not alone. He knew this would comfort Misha.

Misha agreed to meet Neil at the cafe. Sam went a bit early to ensure he was in time and when Misha did not arrive as agreed he waited for a few minutes and then left. Sam did not bother to call Misha and ask what happened.

He did not hear from her for a few days and then weeks past by. Sam got a little bit busy in the office and trying to make more money for himself. He forgot about Misha although not completely, he did still wonder why she never turned up for coffee. One day Partosh came home to discuss some assignment with Ruby. While Partosh was waiting for Ruby, Sam offered a drink and while talking informally enquired about Partosh and his work. Partosh explained about the big client they had recently got and said Ruby was going to be part of this new project too. Sam asked how were things at home and if Misha was getting along well in this town. Partosh was quiet for a few minutes and Sam got worried that maybe Misha had told Partosh. Finally he said, "Misha was not being herself for last few days here. She did not want to talk with me about it but I believe the pressure of living in a big city got to her". She insisted she wanted to go back home and left in a hurry. She is doing much better now and getting back into her own routine at home.

Ruby walked in before they could discuss any further and she apologized for keeping Partosh waiting, Partosh said that Neil was a gentlemen who not only offered him a drink but kept him company too.

Neil asked Ruby if she wanted a drink too but Ruby declined so Neil excused himself and went to look for the kids. Neil found Alexandre running around in his room to dispense off his last bout of energy before going to bed. Neil hugged and kissed Alexandre good night.

He went to check on Laure and found her sleeping peacefully in her crib. With both kids in bed sleeping and Ruby busy with Partosh, Sam felt a bit bored so he took his car and went for a spin. He met Rahim and chatted with him for a while.

He tried to stay away from bars where he knew he could be lured easily into having a few drinks and after that the lure of recreational drugs would be only too easy to fall for again. He was feeling a bit restless so he called Sandra out of the blue and asked if he could visit her. Sandra told Neil he was always welcome at her place. Sam was quite happy to hear this. He liked girls like Sandra who made no fuss. He parked his car in a parking lot close to her house and walked the last few hundred meters. Sam did not need to take such extreme precautions but he always did.

Neil came back home close to 9 pm, and saw Partosh leaving without any supper. He asked Partosh to stay for dinner, although it was a bit late but Partosh declined and excused himself saying he had some work to catch up with.

Neil and Ruby had dinner in silence and then both drifted back to their own world. Ruby went to the bedroom to have her hundred hairbrush strokes and other beauty routines. Neil poured himself a bourbon and went to the patio to enjoy his drink.

Neil came back to the bedroom after finishing his drink and found Ruby watching TV. He changed into his night suit and came to bed. Ruby did not say a word but switched off the TV, turned her back to him and slept. Sam found Ruby a bit subdued but did not question or ask her anything, as he did not want to risk an outburst.

Neil had recently experienced some trouble falling asleep, and even when he did fall asleep he always woke up with nightmares of lot of shouting and people bound in chains, he even saw people in orange prison suits. Neil always woke up before he could recognize anyone or see their faces. He was getting worried if this was a way of destiny pre-warning him.

17

Next morning the Vice President summoned Neil to his office. He said, "A workshop was being planned, to discuss the progress of business plan for the current year and set targets for the next year." Alex asked Neil to prepare a feedback on his projects.

Neil assured him that the time frame of few months was quite adequate for him to get good presentations ready. He assured the Vice President that senior management would be pleased with their progress. Vice President smiled and said there was a surprise but he would not disclose it now. Neil was elated. He was sure he would get nominated as a senior manager in the company.

He left the Vice President's office feeling quite happy and pleased. He was feeling on top of the world in anticipation of the proposed announcement. He left office and went to tell Ruby. He told Ruby the possible good news and for once Ruby seemed genuinely pleased to hear he was going to be elevated to the new position in the company.

Neil started to prepare for the meeting in earnest. He gathered the latest data by emailing and following up with a call to each site manager. He wanted to tell everyone that his hard work was going to be finally recognized.

Sam on the other side was plotting how he would use this new position and gain further leverage and advantage for himself. Neil tried unsuccessfully to shut Sam down but the harder he tried the more energetic and resolved Sam got to use his new position to their advantage. Neil was once again putting long hours in office. Ruby was also getting a bit busy with the new prestigious modeling contract she got. It was a big deal for Ruby, to be able to make a come back after all these years. She was being recognized and received quite well. This gave her more confidence and it appeared her career was finally taking off again.

Ruby arrived home late one evening to find Neil sitting in the dark nursing a glass in his hand. She got worried and asked him what was the matter. Neil broke down and said "You are my life, if you leave me I will not survive." Ruby comforted him "No Alexandre and Laure are your life, I am only a means to that end." Neil told her between sobs, "Never say like that, without you the kids or me will not be able to survive. "

It felt nice to be wanted and loved. Ruby told Neil that she had got another modeling assignment and this was a big deal as she would be contracted for a year and would be an exclusive model for the well known cosmetic brand. Neil was a bit concerned and told her did she really need to stretch herself so much? With the new promotion due soon he could with afford to foot all her bills. Ruby if she wanted, could continue her modeling assignments as a hobby and to satisfy her own career ambition without feeling the pressure of contributing financially to the household. Neil further added, however he would like her to be more mom who is present for the kids rather than a successful model.

Ruby was startled and really annoyed by this attitude of Neil. "I thought you understood my need and desire to be a successful model, but it seemed you are jealous of my success". Neil did not know how to respond to this bolt from the blue. He just mumbled, "I only voiced what I think is best for the kids."

Ruby would have none of this kids blackmail and told him clearly, "I do not neglect the kids and they are your responsibility too. If you think I am not taking good care of them, you are welcome to share the responsibility. She further twisted her knife and asked "By the way do you even know which school or section your son is in?" Without waiting for an answer she stormed out of the room.

Sam was infuriated but he also knew he had to blame himself for this, Sam knew fully well how passionate Ruby was about her career and also how much effort she had put in last six months to reach where she was "a well sought model".

Sam and Ruby had once again started another cold war, both of them lived together but did not speak to each other. In front of family and friends they behaved as if everything was normal but the moment they were alone they clammed up. They were like two strangers each one with an inflated ego and waiting for the other to yield and say sorry. The only person who knew and could see the tension was Nanny. She had seen many such ups and down in this household and knew well how to step carefully around these time bombs.

Nanny did what she did every time Ruby and Neil fought or had an intense argument, she found a quiet place, pulled out her mobile and typed a message about the latest situation in this household and sent the information to her real employer.

○○○

18

Alexandre came back from kindergarten very excited. He had got three golden stars and he wanted to share this. Nanny did not understand any of this stars business but she put on an act for the benefit of Alexandre so that he felt some one is there to share his success. Alexandre has been more well behaved since little Laure came around. He not only was less fussy but he took extremely good care of her. It was fun to watch him take care of her and talk to her. Laure could barely speak some gibberish words but they managed to communicate and laugh together.

Ruby as always was on her phone while driving. She believed she could multi task, drive and text at the same time. She was well aware the traffic was light on the road and possibly was paying more attention to the exchange of SMS messages on her phone with friends. Nice juicy gossip about a common friend got her quite engaged in the exchange of messages. She had an accident, her car collided with an electric pole on the side of the road. She was worried how she would explain this to Neil. Considering the ongoing cold war this could give Neil ammunition he needed. She called the car recovery firm and told them to tow her car to the garage for repairs while she took an Uber.

After having completed her assignment she took a taxi home and was relieved to see Neil was not home yet. She called up the garage and spoke to the mechanic. Ruby told the mechanic to also complete the necessary routine maintenance along with repairs on her car.

Ruby had a quick bath and called out to Alexandre, who ran excitedly to her speaking at a pace, which made it quite difficult to understand. However Ruby got the gist of his talk, that he had got some gold stars and was very happy with his achievement.

Ruby also peeped into Laure's nursery to find her sleeping peacefully, so she took Alexandre in her lap and listened to his stories. It had been a while, since she spent some quality time with him. Ruby did not love children as much as Neil did but she found their company soothing and revitalizing.

Ruby replayed the last argument she had with Neil in her head again; it still got her a bit agitated. How could he be so selfish and self-centered? She had thought Neil worshipped her but in the last few months she had seen a side of him which had shown Neil to be a weak person who has fallen for drugs and even though had managed to clean his act could again fall for it.

Ruby could not let this happen to herself and to her kids. She decided to have a frank talk with Neil and ensure either he understands her viewpoint or was ready to move out of her life. Ruby was aware she still looked drop dead gorgeous and had a brain to match. She had observed men looking at her with desire and lust. She knew she could easily get a husband who would give her all the luxuries of life and secure her future too.

Ruby realized she was so wrapped up in her own thoughts that Alexandre had slept off at some stage in her lap. She called out to the nanny to take Alexandre to bed. She needed a strong drink to have a frank discussion with Neil. Cold War had killed their communication but she needed a resolution.

Ruby knew she was not getting any younger and possibly had a few more years before she would fade away and would be replaced by newer models. She wanted to make these few years count.

Neil staggered into the sitting room and saw Ruby having a drink. Ruby casually asked Neil how was his day. Neil was already a bit high but he poured himself a drink and sat near Ruby. Today he had closed a very good deal for the company and he would only need to formalize the paperwork. Neil was smiling and calculating how much richer he would get personally with this new deal.

Neil then asked Ruby how was she getting on with her new modeling assignments. He realized he had opened the gates for a long discussion when he saw Ruby keep her glass down on the table, turn towards him and say without any hint of smile - "Do not worry about my career, I know what I am doing. It is you I am worried about."

Sam did not know what to make of this caustic remark but he knew tonight would be a long night and he would be sitting here and explaining himself for something he may or may not have done. All the euphoria of having clinched a huge deal suddenly evaporated.

Sam kept his own drink down on the table and looked at Ruby, and finally said, "Let's not be dramatic, I am aware I have made some mistakes in the past but then I have more than paid up for those mistakes so let's not dwell in the past but look at future."

Ruby was not going to loosen her grasp so easily so she said "Past can not be forgotten, your past defines your future". Now Neil knew whatever Ruby was going to say was important and he needed to up his game if he hoped to survive this discussion with no permanent wounds.

Ruby told Neil that she wanted to leave him. She said this was not a spontaneous decision but she had thought about it carefully and seriously she was well aware that they share the kids but she cannot live with a man who does not respect her choice of career or what she does. Sam who was quiet till now went ballistic with a desire to reprimand her behavior with great fury and he said "You only think about yourself and your career. Do you have any idea what I have to put up with?"

The moment the words left Sam's mouth he immediately regretted it, he knew this was not a good idea. Being offensive with Ruby when she was already cross was never a good idea. He realized it would be a long discussion and he would have to apologize at the end else there would be no peace.

Ruby just exploded as expected, she said "Yeah you face all the hardships and I am supposed to be the selfish one? You need to look at yourself while I was pregnant and otherwise too I know about all your "other" fun activities so don't you ever lecture me about being selfish or anything else." Ruby took a deep breath and continued "You were a nobody till I decided to marry you and hold your hand. Don't forget I gave you the idea about this I am the one who invested and had faith in you when you yourself did not even believe in your abilities. You worthless piece of wreck, you drank yourself silly and got into drugs but I still stood by your side and supported you when you needed me." Ruby once on the roll did not need much to bring up everything from Neil's own shortcomings to his poor background, to his parents and everything else whether justified or not. Neil knew it and had still lit that fuse, so now he had no choice but to face the music.

Finally, after a long speech Ruby asked Neil, "Do you have anything to say or will you once again say sorry which you never mean and believe that everything has been resolved and we can go back to being a happy couple". Neil had a lot to say but as always he knew it was better not to add more fuel to the fire. He did what he thought would bring peace in the house and get him out of this emotional mess.

Neil apologized which was anyway expected of him and then excused himself and left for a walk outside in the cold air. He felt a bit throttled and was frustrated by all the humiliation once again including demeaning of his family and calling him names. He could never forget when he was called names for the first time and he has tried to wave a white flag and get some peace. Since then all he had done was wave a white flag.

Neil wanted to scream but he did not want to attract attention of his neighbors or wake up the kids so he went to the car garage and screamed within.., he could never repent enough why he had married or agreed to put up with Ruby. Sam knew he was not afraid of her and neither did he care about the society or what others thought of him but he cared about his two little angels and all the sacrifice he was making was only to ensure they did grow up as normal children and not the ones from a broken home.

Sometimes he did wonder if this was an excuse for himself or did he even really think that his kids would not adapt if ever needed. He was not sure and wished he would never have to find out.

Sam was getting jittery with this new and sudden announcement from Ruby. All his planning and schedule was going haywire. He had to fast track his plans, he did not want Ruby to leave him and make him the butt of all jokes. He was well aware of the jokes circulating about him in the office and friend's circle.

Sam started to blame Ruby instead, he started saying to himself that Ruby was jealous of his success and cannot see anyone else succeeding besides herself. The recent success of Ruby as a model had made her too self-centered and all Ruby can see and talk about was herself. She would not leave any opportunity to belittle anyone else specially Neil. The more Sam repeated this the more he believed it to be true.

The gulf between Ruby and Neil was widening at a very fast pace and it seemed they would go their separate ways soon. The situation was impossible to live with; a life full of constant stress and fights with each of them trying to find a way to belittle or mock the other at every opportunity.

While all this was unfolding, Ruby had her sister visiting them after ages. Emerald had not been able to come to help Ruby during Laure's birth and she felt guilty about it. Emerald called up Ruby one day and told her that she was going to visit them next week. Before even Ruby could react she disconnected the phone. Ruby tried to call up Emerald and explain to her not to come but Emerald would not have any of that.

Emerald landed at her house on a sunny day bursting with energy. Alexandre was joyous and full of laughter as he remembered her last visit a while back, when she had come with loads of toys for him. How she would throw him up in the air and catch him, Alexandre loved it.

Neil and Ruby called it truce and tried to put up a picture of a happy family. However, the sisters when alone shared with each other their true feeling. Ruby told Emerald how she and Neil were on the verge of getting separated. Emerald was shocked to hear this, she had always thought Neil and Ruby were the ideal couple and both were happy.

Emerald tried to ask Ruby to reconsider her decision and to give Neil another chance. Emerald also told Neil maybe they both - Ruby and Neil are unduly stressed with the fast pace of their life and need a bit of time together away from the kids and other responsibilities.

Emerald insisted Ruby to book a weekend holiday in the country. She promised to take care of the kids. Ruby was initially a bit reluctant but after hearing all the arguments and pleading from her sister, Ruby relented and agreed to book a holiday as a surprise for Neil.

Neil although still a bit hurt from the constant barbs of his wife was pleased that Ruby had taken this step to try to bridge the gap between them. He thought of it as an olive branch from Ruby and agreed. In his heart he was a bit excited to have even a weekend away from kids and home. He wanted to be alone with Ruby and pamper her to ensure she did not leave him just yet.

With few days to plan or reverse the decision the excitement and the energy of Emerald did not let them back out. On Friday afternoon Neil and Ruby left the kids with

Emerald and drove off with lot of anticipation from this weekend together.

Ruby had booked the best country club within driving distance. They took a short coffee break on the way and arrived at the picturesque country club. The king suite which Ruby had booked was a treat with a personal butler and their own maid to cater to all their whims.

Once they entered the reception of the hotel their bags disappeared and they were given a welcome drink and a guided tour of the facility so that they could enjoy their stay in the club to the fullest.

After the tour when they came to their suite, they found their bags unpacked and arranged in the wardrobe, their night suits laid out on the dresser and ironed. The beds turned down and a bottle of complimentary champagne from the hotel at the table.

Although not trying to look impressed, Sam was actually mighty impressed by Ruby's arrangements. He hugged Ruby and thanked her for her thoughtful gesture. They both had a quick shower and sat down to enjoy the bottle of champagne with a romantic movie in the sitting room.

Before even the movie started Neil dared Ruby that he would do everything the hero does and asked if Ruby was game to do as the leading lady did. Ruby who was not going to go down without a fight agreed. Both of them thought it would be fun.

Soon enough Neil was acting his heart out along with the hero on the TV and even Ruby who was quite not herself for last few days forgot all her worries and joined in. Both of then enjoyed the bottle of champagne and small snacks while enacting the movie scenes and laughing at themselves. It felt quite nice and refreshing to be able to forget everything else in the world even though only for a weekend.

Neil and Ruby had a great Saturday too, got up leisurely, had their breakfast in bed, followed by a spa treatment and a luxurious time at the pool. Finally in the afternoon they went for a walk and came back a bit late and missed the evening show at the bar, but after a long time they were enjoying each other's company and did not mind being left to themselves.

Sunday also started on similar lines as Saturday but as they checked out and headed back to their life in town they each vowed to make an effort to try and mend whatever was broken in their relationship, if not for their sake but for the sake of their children.

Alexandre was delighted to see them back and had so many stories to tell. It seemed they had never been away. Ruby thanked Emerald for her great suggestion and told her the trip was a real stress buster and got her ready for another year of endless strict regime which she would need to follow to ensure she remained in business.

Emerald asked her sister - "I know this is really important for you to be successful and well recognized for your work but is this enough? Don't you think a successful life is where kids remember you and not some random people, who will soon forgot you and move on to the next new model who comes along in a few years?"

Emerald the elder sibling was always mature beyond her age. She had actually been a wild kid in the college and soon afterwards married while she was still working on her final thesis. By the time, she finished her thesis the relationship too had fizzled out. She got divorced soon thereafter.

The next few years saw her having a few serious hook ups but she never married again and as Emerald would say, each of her relationship were an education and taught her more about life than anyone could ever teach her.

Emerald had learnt about different nationalities, their cultures, their favorite cuss words and tried out different cuisines, all the traveling around the world had made her headstrong and worldly wise. Unfortunately, it also made her to not get attached to anyone anymore. Emerald rarely let anyone get close to her; however she always found solace with Ruby.

Ruby was always the sister with beauty and brains, and at some point in her teens Emerald had hated Ruby, but then she realized they might be different to look at but inside both of them were quite similar. After the divorce Emerald was a wreck and this was the time when Ruby showed strong character and steadied the ship for Emerald. Emerald had a miscarriage and she blamed her husband for it. He was an alcoholic anyway but he pushed Emerald while she was 8 months pregnant in a fit of rage, she tripped and fell down. She lay in a pool of blood till a neighbor who happened to like Emerald and used to spend time with her came over. He saw the mess and called an ambulance but it was too late. The miscarriage started the slide, which tore the relationship apart and possibly it was a good thing for Emerald. She was far too young and immature to be stuck with an alcoholic who was at least a decade older than she was and relied on her for funding even his drinking habit.

The sisters after that unfortunate incident had stayed in touch and offered each other emotional support, which made their bond strong. Emerald stayed for another few days and then left with a promise to return soon.

Lately Alexandre has been quite attached to his dad. He could see his dad as the super hero who could do anything. Every weekend he systematically pulled out all the toys he managed to wreck in the week and asked Neil to help with repairing them. Neil could never say no to Alexandre and tried his best to make sure if not all most of Alexandre favorite toys were working again. Sometimes he cheated and bought a similar toy from the market and gave to Alexandre, who thought his dad had repaired it.

Ruby was never too involved in Alexandre or Laure, she left them to be taken care of by the nanny. She had much more important things to do. Its not that she did not care but she was not an emotional and possessive mom, she left most of the daily chores to the nanny but spend some quality time with them whenever she could spare some time from her modelling aspirations.

19

A 35 year old Neil is a busy senior manager in his company. He is "*happily*" married and lives with his wife and two kids in an upcoming suburb. Today is the day he had waited for a long time. The words of Vice President ring in his ears, " I have a surprise for you but I will not disclose it now".

Neil came early to the meeting room, hooked up his laptop, and had already skimmed through his slides to make sure he was on top of the topics he would be talking about. He wanted today to be a grand success and was looking forward to a much-anticipated promotion.

Within minutes, almost all the chairs were taken in the room. The Vice President opened the meeting and thanked the chairman for coming over for this meeting. Next he announced the agenda of the meeting and once again said that he had some very good news but he would deliver it at the end of the meeting. Everyone murmured and joked about having an enormous bonus or out of turn increment.

The next few hours passed in a flash with the finance manager giving the company financial accounts, profit and loss statement, followed by a vision statement by the HSE manager. Then Neil gave an impressive presentation about the progress of his projects and showed various graphs, some of which were a little skewed, to impress the management. Lastly the IT manager gave a review of future improvements planned on servers and hardware upgrades and the road map for it.

Now once again all eyes were on the Vice President expectantly, who just smiled and picked up the intercom, and said "Yes, send him in" and kept the phone back on cradle. He then said, "The news which you all have been impatiently waiting for - I present to you the new Projects GM of our company" and after a dramatic pause added – "Mr. Scott". This news stunned everyone and most of all Sam who could not believe what he had just heard. When he heard Projects GM, he was preparing to get up once his name was announced but even in his wildest imagination he did not expect this.

The door of the meeting room opened and Scott walked in, hail and hearty, as if he never had the accident. Most of the members got up to shake hands with him. Up close one could see a few faint scars which would remind who knew Scott from before about his accident. Scott met everyone and last but not the least Neil who somehow struggled to get up from his chair. He too congratulated Scott and was about to move out of the room following most of other people who had left the room or were leaving, when Scott called him, "Neil please do not be too long, I need to speak to you".

Sam was very confused and disturbed, he had never expected this and now felt like kicking himself for not keeping in touch with Scott for the last few months, else he would have known this development, but he could not understand how he did not pick up messages being sent or calls being made to Scott's mobile phone.

He rushed to Scott's cabin and picking up his laptop opened his spy program. Nothing looked astray. It seemed the log was recent and so was the email folder too with a few recent emails. Sam was really frustrated and angry.

He had to go back and speak to Scott. Later he would get to the bottom of this problem of missing emails and phone calls. Sam went back to the meeting room to find only Scott , the legal manager, Human Resource manager and Vice president in the room.

Scott invited Neil to sit down. Once Neil was seated,. Scott started the dialogue with a statement which completely rattled Neil - "You are no longer required in this company and can either resign or I will fire you".

Neil looked up at all the faces and realized this was all staged for his benefit and the decision had already been taken. The HR manager spoke firmly and said- "If you do not resign today I will be starting an investigation into all your project work since you took over Scott's portfolio. However if you choose to resign the company will accept your resignation with immediate effect and you would be escorted out of this building with your personal belongings in an hour".

Neil looked at the Vice President and then at Scott, Neil's face must have shown his surprise and confusion because Scott answered his question- "I am aware and everyone here too is aware of your project work arrangements and also your personal benefits derived so there is no point in speaking and trying to defend your position."

Neil asked the Vice President, "Sir, you too want me to resign?" The Vice President looked up from his laptop and said, "Neil, it is not Scott's decision, this has been carefully discussed and Board has agreed to let you go. You should be thankful that Scott is your friend and insisted we let you go with dignity." Neil had never dreamt it would turn out this way. He looked outside the frosted glass partition and felt as if everyone was gossiping about him and his departure.

True to his word the HR manager arranged for two guards to escort Neil out of the meeting room to Scott's office to pack his things. Once he collected his things, the security escorted him out of the building while Neil tried to balance the backpack he was carrying and a cardboard box with his meagre belongings. Eventually, he had to keep the box at the reception to adjust his backpack. The ever-smiling receptionist quickly averted his eyes and excused herself from her seat.

Sam could see the receptionist talking to a few other office staff and saw them looking in his direction, it appeared to him that they were all discussing him. Sam was getting furious with this treatment meted out to him but then he had no one he could blame.

Sam vented some of his frustration by mouthing a few expletives for all his past colleagues before making way to the main door and handing his ID card to the security guard. The guard seemed to be wearing a smirk on his face. Sam had to control his temper and restrain himself from having a go at him. Sam held the security guard with his collar in his hand but better sense prevailed for once in his life and he let go of him. It was better to move to his car and leave this place as quickly as possible.

Neil got into his car, dropped his bag and the cardboard box on the front passenger seat and started his car. Sam took a deep breath and smiling inwardly drove off.

Sam decided not to go home immediately, he knew the moment he would tell Ruby, she would freak out. She will not think logically and in all probability he would be blamed, accused and abused. Neil was upset but Sam wanted to understand how he had not seen it coming. Sam decided to check into a hotel, calm down, plan his next move, and then go home.

Sam took a U-turn and headed to the south west side of the town, he was aware of many hotels close to the airport which were not pricey and with constant flow of people busy enough for him to slip in and out. Sam drove with his hands holding the steering wheel so tight that his knuckles were white.

Neil arrived and swung into the first hotel he saw. He went to the reception and asked for a room, he checked in using his own credit card. He took the room key and went to his room. The eerie silence in the room was driving him crazy so he switched on the news channel on television and went to wash his face.

Neil heard the name of his company and came back quickly to see what was on the news, and to his shock, the Vice President was on television and answering questions about board meeting held a few hours back. His heart sank, although not a religious person for once he prayed, please God don't let him reveal the news of what happened to me. He could have asked for any other wish and probably that could be granted to him but not this one, soon enough one of the reporter from a famous tabloid asked about changes in the management. The Vice President told that Mr.Scott who had suffered quite a serious accident and was out of our company due to medical reasons has joined back and he has been elevated to the post of Projects GM. Another reporter asked about sacking of Mr.Neil and then the Vice President said, "Mr.Neil has decided to pursue other ventures and our company mutually agreed with him to part ways".

The news reporter was cut off and they returned to the newsroom and then the newsroom debate started about what did this mean, how it was quite strange for Scott to be coming back after such a long break and getting elevated to the new position. One of the panelists said - "If there is smoke there must be fire, there is more to sacking of Neil than what the company representative told us and we should follow up to get the bottom of this in the next few days". He flipped to another business Channel and there he was on the screen with some reporter giving another spicy story of how he has been let go by the company.

Neil's phone was ringing non-stop as different people, some from the media and others who had colluded with him on projects; were trying to get in touch with him. What could Neil tell them? He just removed the battery from his phone and threw it on the bed.

Neil slumped down in the chair holding his head in his hands. He needed a drink badly. He opened the mini bar and saw two single shots of whisky inside. Without any delay he twisted open the seal and just drained both the bottles into his mouth. The alcohol burnt his throat, however it was nothing compared to what his heart was feeling right now.

Neil did not want to go down to the bar and be seen by other people, he dialed room service and asked for a bottle of whisky to be delivered to his room. He needed some alcohol to calm him down and he could always think of how he would deal with the crisis in his life tomorrow. The door bell rang and the waiter came in with the bottle of whisky, Neil signed his bill and the wide eyes of the waiter said it all. Sam pushed some money into the waiter's hand and told him to keep it quiet that he was here. The waiter nodded and left.

Sam heard some commotion and woke up to hear the phone ringing, and before he could even answer the phone, his room door bell was ringing. He looked around and remembered he was not in his house but in a hotel. Yesterday incident flooded back in his memory, his head was bursting but he could guess who would be at the door. The waiter must have crooned to someone. He got up and staggered to the door and looked through the keyhole to see a cameraman and a reporter outside his door.

Neil did not answer the doorbell but called up reception and asked for the manager. He spoke to the manager and told him to move these people from outside his room. The manager whom Sam knew from his previous stays in the hotel when he needed to be discreet, promised to help him. After about half an hour the manager called back and told Neil that he had moved them from his floor but they were camping outside the hotel close to Neil's car. If Neil wanted to leave he could use the back door as an escape and get his car picked up later. Neil thanked him and asked him to arrange for a taxi.

An hour later Neil arrived home and paid for the taxi in his driveway. He tried to open the automatic garage door but it did not function. He cursed under his breath, got out of the taxi and walked to the main door. He took his keys out to open the door, but the key wouldn't fit in the lock. He looked at the door again. Nothing seemed to have been disturbed but he did notice the new lock barrel.

Sam mouthed a few more curses, shouted and kicked the door in frustration. He rang the door bell, no answer, he tried it again, no answer. He walked around to the back door, tried the back door, that too was locked. He tried to peep in but could not see much with all curtains drawn. The house seemed to be empty.

Sam walked again to the front door, then realized possibly the kids and Ruby could have gone to the local market. Maybe the cook and Nanny had gone with them. Sam decided to call Ruby on her mobile phone. The phone kept ringing but no answer. While he disconnected and was about to dial again, he got a message – "Don't ever call me again, you will get the divorce papers by mail - Ruby".

Sam could not believe what he had just read, the screen had turned blank, He opened his messages again and re-read the message out to himself aloud. He let out a laugh and then turned to look at the house. In a fit of rage Sam threw the phone at the door. The glass shattered and the anti-theft alarm started to ring. He moved closer to the main door and tried to snake in his hand to unlock the front door.

The shrill sound had got the attention of a few neighbors and they were either out and watching him or trying to see what he was doing from behind their curtains. Sam did not care, after a few tries he managed to grab the lever and turn it to unlock the door. Sam got in and even before he could close his door, Sam heard the siren of a police car.

Sam froze and started to panic, but then he realized this was his own house so he need not need panic. The police car screeched to a halt outside his door, two policemen purposefully but cautiously walked towards the house with their weapons drawn. The third policemen picked up a loud hailer and made an announcement for him to come out with his heads visible.

Sam just screamed "SCREW YOU" loudly and slammed the door. Sam's head was buzzing with loud noise of the alarm and not to mention the excessive alcohol he had consumed last night. Sam approached the alarm panel and input the code, a caution flashed on the screen "wrong pin code!!!", Sam thought to himself WHAT THE HELL IS GOING ON…!!, he tried it again but the same message flashed again and the alarm sound would not stop.

Sam was losing his temper now, he picked up a vase from the foyer table and raised it above his head to hit the alarm panel with it, when he heard - "Police, freeze, keep the vase down turn around and walk with both your hands visible slowly to the door. Sam mouthed another cuss word but before he could move his arm a bullet was fired and he was hit on his finger, he screamed and dropped the vase.

Sam was delirious now, he was screaming loudly and competing with the shrill sound of the alarm. The policemen moved in swiftly, pinned him down and handcuffed him while reading him his rights. He was roughly pushed back to his feet and the policemen silenced the alarm.

While Neil was brought out of his house he noticed the local TV crew all set to get a new sensational story. Neil tried to hide behind the policemen escorting him and make himself invisible but a mic was thrust into his face and someone shouted to him, "Can you tell us why you broke into the house?" Thankfully, the police pushed the media persons away while news hungry vultures kept taking pictures and rolling video recording every single move Sam made on their camera. Someone has possibly given the scoop and he heard his name been said and then a bizarre story about him.

Sam who was usually in control of situations or knew how to react, suddenly felt helpless. He was roughly pushed in a police van. Sam had read stories about how first time prisoners were treated in the prison and he started to tremble. He had no desire to find out if what he has read or seen in movies about prison was true.

He started thinking how he could get out of this tricky situation. All he remembered was that the company sacked him and to avoid barbed comments from Ruby he had gone to a hotel to lay low; keep out of harms way at home, professional and public fronts. He remembered ordering a drink but strangely nothing more from the point he started to drink till he woke up this morning.

20

Sam was on the way to the police station thinking hard who all he could call to ensure he got a bail as soon as possible. He could not think of spending even a single night in the jail. In his mind he had not committed any crime so he did not understand why he was arrested and being taken to local police station.

Finally, they reached the station, his hands were freed, and he was allowed to make a call. Sam called up his lawyer and requested him to come immediately and ensure he got bail. Today was friday and if the bail was not granted today he would be left in police remand till monday. The lawyer assured him he would do everything possible to ensure that Neil got the bail. Sam also asked him to contact his wife Ruby and find out what happened. The lawyer did not argue with him and this was the kind of people Sam liked. People who did what they are told without getting into details. After having spoken to his lawyer suddenly, Sam felt a sense of relief.

The relief was short lived, as he waited for hours but never got a message or his bail papers. With the failing sunlight, his hope of getting out of this local station was also fading. Although he silently hoped the lawyer would come soon but with no information of what progress has been made and where the lawyer was, all he had left was hope.

The police station in charge came and appraised him that if his lawyer did not come back with the bail papers in the next hour, Neil would have no option but to stay till Monday here in the local lock up. To Sam it seemed as if the person was not telling him but mocking him. He requested if he could make another phone call but that was declined on grounds that he had already exhausted his quota of phone calls.

Finally, the papers did not come and he was photographed, bathed and given the orange coverall; same as all others in the prison were wearing. Sam saw some real big fellows with lot of tattoos, bulging muscles, visible scars and missing teeth looking with interest at him. Neil cringed internally; he did not know what he could do and how he would survive. Suddenly the images from his past dreams with police cars, prison came alive and it all seemed so surreal. He would have never ever guessed that all those dreams were about him.

Neil was put in a cell with three other inmates, all of them waiting for their lawyers to get their bail papers. Neil tried to keep to himself but the room was small and it was difficult to tune yourself out with the noise and constant chatter between different people. At some stage weariness took over and he fell asleep.

It did not last for long, he heard some noises and woke up to loud snoring from two of his inmates, the sound itself was disturbing enough but when the amplitudes matched the resonance was quite jarring. Neil could not sleep, he lay in the smelly so called mattress wide-awake and could now clearly see and recall that the hazy person he saw in his dreams was Neil himself. This was one of those dreams that he had few times every year but it was never clear what happened before or after this.

Neil had seen this so many times without realizing he was looking at his future. He tried to figure out the face but in dream it was always hazy and not clear. Neil saw the young guy on the upper bunk was also having a lot of difficulty to get sleep. Neil gestured to the guy to come down from his bunk. The guy completely ignored him. Sam was seething with anger but he knew well if he would have reacted to it the little advantage he had would be lost and not to mention he would be beaten to pulp. Neil wanted to get out but at this time everywhere he would go Sam would be dodging all those different people who all seemed to be happy and used Sam to invest their money in past but today did not want to see or hear from him. Sam was quite aware that in this world you suffer alone and people when they laugh they laugh at you rather than laugh with you.

Sam saw this time as an opportunity to make some quick easy money. He started to plot how to attract attention of the heavy weights in the lock up to give him the money with a promise that he can easily give them generous profits. All he had to do was to get enough money so that he could escape to his dream island where no one knew him. Sam started to think how he could take their money without leaving a trace. Neil meanwhile was busy thinking how he would survive the next two days in this hellhole and if he would be alive on Monday morning.

Saturday morning Sam tried to explain to people that to make money you need to spend money and invest wisely. Someone shouted from across the room to not give a lecture on how to invest and where to invest. The man further added the only way to make fast and easy money was to cheat others.

Neil was a famous prison inmate, most of the inmates in prison had seen him on TV and they all wanted to be rich and famous without doing hard work. Sam usually did not relate to these cell inmates but he had 48 hours to find a way to win their confidence to hand over their money to invest and multiply. Sam knew this was an opportunity to swindle some money from other greedy people.

He managed to convince the person in his cell that he can convert money into a profit-making machine; Sam always had a gift of convincing people. The big man came to him and asked him if Neil would take care of his money. Neil did not want to get involved but greed glittered and blinded Sam who would do anything to make some easy money. You can call it easy money when you are trying to steal from people who had already stolen it from someone else.

Sam had a plan to get them to agree and invest with him but not to share any profit. This was a dangerous game to play but Sam liked playing with danger. The big fellow told him whom to contact to get the money once Neil was outside for investing.

Sam was enjoying his stay now since he was getting to add more to his money making machine, all Sam wanted was money. He was not a person who liked expensive clothes or flashy cars. He was a man who liked to amass wealth, the only time he spent any money was to get into someone's pants. That too he felt was not worth it but he did it more out of habit now.

This was a slippery slope and Sam related it akin to getting taste of blood. Like a lion once having tasted blood becomes a man-eater, same was the case with Sam. He could not keep his pants zipped up. If he saw a girl he had to pursue her and get her to bed. Not that he had not experienced failures in his endeavours, he had, but he was a quick learner and now he did not chase the best-looking girls in the room. He chased the second best and waited for the best ones to approach him.

Sam's lawyer managed to get him out of prison on Monday, the papers were all signed by 1100 hours but by the time order was released, it was lunch time and then getting the formalities completed, by the time Neil managed to change into his own clothes and left the prison door it was close to 4 pm.

Sam felt the time in prison was productive and effective as it not only gave him some contacts who could be useful in future but also a channel to take some money from other people.

Once out, Sam did not know what to do, he had still not found the answer why the locks of his house were changed and why Ruby has behaving this way. He was going to find out.

The lawyer asked Neil if he wanted to be dropped at any place. Neil asked him to drop him at a place from where he can get a cab. The prison was on the outskirts of the town and was not very well connected. The lawyer asked him if he had any specific place in mind where he could drop him but Neil said "No thanks, if you can drop me to the nearby commercial centre; where I can find some transport, I will manage from there.

He knew everyone knew by now that he was not even welcome at his house but he was going to change it. He was going to go home and give Ruby some lesson in being supportive when things go wrong. Sam was outwardly calm but inside he felt like a raging bull.

Sam took a taxi home, while he approaching his house he saw a familiar car in the driveway. He had no intention to meet or speak to Scott. He held Scott fully responsible for what happened to him. If Scott would have wanted he could have avoided all of this, It seemed to Sam that Scott was punishing him for marrying Ruby and taking the love of his life away from him. How Sam wished he could tell Scott that Ruby was never there for him. Ruby lived only for herself then and even now. Ruby was the reason for Sam's downfall. If she would have agreed to share her newfound wealth, Sam would not have to go down the path he went to get rich quickly.

Sam could give all the possible excuses for everything but Neil knew it was GREED, which made Sam what he had, become. How Neil wished he could control Sam if not fully but especially when he was running berserk but alas he had little or no control over this other half.

Sam paid the taxi with the money he had borrowed from his lawyer, who was kind enough to loan him a hundred for his immediate needs. Sam walked towards the house but something told him not to go from the front door. He walked around to the back yard and peeped in from the window while hiding behind a pillar.

What he saw shocked him. Ruby was sitting with a cup of tea and crying. Scott stood behind her and had his hands on her shoulders which made Sam very angry. He could not hear anything but Neil stood and watched them. It seemed Ruby was quite stressed and gesturing with her hands while Scott was trying to calm her down.

Neil did not know how long he stood there and watched but it seemed like a life time. He saw Scott help Ruby to get up and hold her closely while walking her to her bedroom. Near the stairs they lingered for a while and then Scott and Ruby kissed, first a bit awkwardly but then more passionately. This was a bit too much to watch for Sam. He started to scream, picked up a stone and threw it at the dining room window.

The noise and commotion made Scott and Ruby turn and look directly at him. Sam ran to the kitchen door and found it to be open. He opened the door and ran towards the stairs. He met Scott near the dining room door; Scott seemed calm and collected which fueled Sam's anger more.

Sam ran straight at Scott and tried to head butt him but Scott was ready. He moved to the side and pushed Sam towards the door. Sam like a charging bull could not stop himself and ran into the opposite door with full force. Sam shook the heavy teak door right upto its hinges but ended up on the floor holding his head in both hands.

All his energy seemed to have drained from him. He did not know if it was the ringing in his head or someone had called the local enforcement again. He tried to get up but ended up doubling up on the floor and throwing up his breakfast all over the floor.

Scott came around dragged him with his arm to the bathroom while firing a few expletives at him and threw him in the shower with all his clothes on. The cold water initially jarred his nerves but then got his focus back. He was struggling to breath, and moved his head away from the stream of water jet.

Scott threw a towel at him and told Neil to dry himself up and then change into something dry. Scott instructed him to come out after changing and then they would discuss this as mature adults. Neil had no fight left in him and he still needed the answers from Ruby.

Neil got up and went to his room to change. Ruby and Scott stayed put in the sitting room waiting for his return. On the way up the stairs, he heard the maid being instructed to clean up the mess in the dining room and then take the kids to the park.

For a moment, Neil panicked about what the plan of Ruby and Scott was now. Sam was wondering if they were going to corner him and force him to give away the details of his hidden stash and then kill him? Sam was very sure he had kept his secret stash separate from Ruby and Ruby had no clue of its existence. Neil tried to think of what else it could be that they had to say for which the maid was being made to go away.

While in his room, he locked the door from inside and pulled a chair under the handle so that it could not be opened from the other side. He took his clothes off while continuously glancing over his shoulder to see if he was going to be attacked. Suddenly Sam felt he has been cornered like a rat with nowhere to run.

He quickly managed to change into a casual T shirt and a pair of jeans and then proceeded to quietly unlock the door. After making sure that no one was hiding in the hall way to ambush him he tip toed towards the stairs. There was an eerie silence and he as quietly as he could descended to the sitting room. He saw Ruby sitting in his Victorian chair with high back and Scott standing next to her and both talking in low whispers.

Once he arrived, Ruby gestured towards him, which made Scott also turn around and face him. Surprisingly, it was Scott who addressed him, Scott invited Neil to take a chair and sit down. Scott told him to feel free and have a glass of water, and only water as he wanted Neil to have a clear head and listen very carefully what Scott had to say.

Before even Neil could open his mouth, Ruby almost pounced on him, slapped him on his face and then kicked him in the shin. Sam looked at her with eyes full of hatred and moved to get up and reciprocate with some punches but Scott told him not to even dream about it.

Scott said to Neil, you deserve a lot worse than what has been meted out to you so far and now since you are here let me tell you a little story.

Scott started from the time of his accident. He recapped the accident and how Neil was initially very helpful, which Scott needed at that time. Scott further added, for that Scott would always stay indebted to him but what happened after that washed all that good deed away.

Scott said I never expected you to become who you became, your greed and desire to rise exponentially made you become a person of no morals or human affection. Scott further added if you are wondering what I am saying is not true I leave you to judge but I will not leave you in peace if you ever try to harm anyone whom I care for.

Scott started to recount - Initially in the hospital on that bed while I waited for a miracle or two you were busy plotting how to displace me. I would not have possibly ever known except you kept giving me reasons to keep thinking why you were behaving the way you were.

When you removed the project manager after the accident on the site, you must have thought he left without a trace. He did not leave immediately he came to me and told me what exactly happened and how you managed to blame him for everything. He wanted to put up a fight but I knew from our discussions that you had managed to manipulate the situation and mould most of the people to listen to you.

Even at that time, I thought you were possibly a bit misguided and were only doing this to ensure that the company's reputation does not suffer. I wish I had stopped you then. I gave you benefit of doubt and a long rope and you finally managed to put a noose around your own neck.

Scott said – "I had a few favors which people owned me, I called one of my friends and told him to employ our project manager and vouched for his honesty. You literally ruined that man's career for your own ambition. Neil that time, when I should have seen you as a monster but I did not. I do blame myself for what everyone around me had to suffer. I did try to save them but I did not want you to know that I knew or was doing some things to alter your plans.

I always thought you were a good friend and were doing everything to help me, my family and Ruby. However, when Ruby came to me few months back and told me that you have changed and greed is your middle name now, I asked her to tell me everything she knew. She was very sad and was on the verge of ending her life but could not come to do it because of the children.

Scott was facing Neil but Neil was watching Ruby. Neil noticed the twinkle of win in her eyes and that little smile on her lips as if mocking Neil. Sam was extremely angry but he had been outplayed by a woman who was smarter than him and knew well how to manipulate men.

Neil told Scott to stop and to listen to him, Sam wanted to tell Scott how Ruby was the one who duped Scott and planned the whole thing with Neil. Before Neil could even start to speak, Scott told him I know what you are going to say Neil, you want to tell me how all this was planned by Ruby and how she made you marry her. Ruby has already warned me you would say so.

Scott said, I have not known you long enough but I have known her for little while longer and especially how she collaborated with me, helped me to understand your plan. I do not think anything you would say can change my mind. Scott also mentioned that Ruby told him how Neil mistreated Scott's son Alexandre.

Neil was totally taken aback how deep rooted Ruby plan was and how well she had planned the whole operation. Sam screamed out loud- "Your son Scott!!??, if you were so intelligent you would have got a DNA test done." Scott just looked at Neil, smiled and said we did get the test done and I have the result he is my son. Ruby is the one who suggested that we get the test done to establish whose son Alexandre was. Ruby is the one who took appointments, arranged for the test, and even made sure that doctor calls me to deliver the result personally to me.

Neil looked at Ruby and saw the smirk on her face which was telling him "Stupid man you do not know whom you got involved with. You have no idea." Sam suddenly was crestfallen and it dawned upon him that Ruby had not only outplayed him once but at every move.

Scott carried on, Scott told Neil once Ruby informed me few months back that you had my phone rigged, I got a new phone and then onward you only saw on that phone what I wanted you to see. I was still recovering but your betrayal gave me a resolve to gain strength and stand on my own feet so that I can stand face to face with you. I wanted to see the look on your face when you hear that I knew.

Scott told him how he planted the housemaid in his house with a little assistance from Ruby. Once the maid was there she used to keep Scott informed of all what was going on in the house. Sam was thinking to himself the maid was probably getting some help from Ruby too so that she can convey what Ruby wanted to be conveyed to Scott.

Scott told Neil, the housemaid used to bring little Alexandre to Scott's place at times. This gave Scott some time alone with his son to bond with him. Scott also told Neil how the housemaid used to make video and sent it to him on so that Scott did not miss any important moments of his son.

Now it was all coming back to Neil, how Ruby insisted on this housemaid only to be employed and how she made excuses that they needed her so that Ruby could start her own life. Neil wanted to ask Scott if Ruby was also meeting him behind Neil's back. But Neil did not want to hear the truth, he knew in all probability since Ruby stopped talking or discussing about Scott, she was meeting him regularly and knew almost everything Neil knew or possibly much more about Scott's progress during the recovery phase.

Neil felt like kicking his own backside that how he could not see or understand why she never really asked him about Scott and she suddenly developed a keen interest in his work for the last few months whereas earlier she never used to bother with it except to know how much money she could spent.

Scott seemed to be enjoying watching Neil get uncomfortable. Scott continued on and told Neil, "I am sure you would be really surprised to know and maybe this may even surprise Ruby a bit, I knew you had my phone rigged when the project manager came to me much before Ruby even told me. The Project Manager had warned me about you and told me to be extremely careful about. The project manager visited me few months back and we were discussing work.

"I had defended you and told him about how honest and sincere you have been, and showed him the new phone you got for me, this is when he said this phone looks strange. We have only black iPhones in the company and yours is white. I told him maybe they ran out of black ones. However I left it without any further thought. When Ruby told me, I called up the IT manager and asked him about my phone. He asked for serial number and then confirmed to me that the phone was not purchased by the company but you personally.

This whole phone situation looked very strange to me, so I called the IT manager home and gave the phone to him for investigation. He monitored it for two days and came back with the list of unauthorized and masked programs you had installed for monitoring and copying my phone. With his contacts he managed to find out which retailer you purchased the phone from but you were smart you did not buy it yourself directly but employed someone else to buy it for you. I am sure if I would have tried to confront you, you would have played the innocent victim. You, Mr. Neil would have found a way to blame the intermediate dealer and put him also in big trouble like the project manager during that incident on site.

"If I was not fighting the battle for my own survival and recovery I would have found a way to make you accountable for your deeds till then which was only a short list at that time. However I had little energy to do anything else except keep afloat myself. I am sure you noticed how I stopped talking to you about work. Of course, you too stopped giving me any news soon after the site incident. I had by then lost a little bit of faith in you. However, the goodness in me did not see the monster in you. I only regret that I failed to notice you were like a cancer spreading not only in my life but in the company and lives of Ruby, Alexandre and everyone else."

Scott was a little breathless and tired of standing so he poured a glass of water, drank a little bit water then sat down near Ruby and continued to talk to Neil. Scott told Neil that if nothing else the gesture of Ruby to come and tell Scott that his phone was rigged showed whose side she was on. It became very easy to trust her since she had earned it.

Neil was shaking his head and mumbling to himself but Scott told him, "Once I am done with you, you will have years to ponder over the past. Scott further added, "I normally do not ponder over the past but you would because I would make sure you have no future; And this I would do to repent my past error in judgement.

Scott continued, There are many more things that me and Ruby know but you have little to no knowledge of it. Neil looked a bit worried. Scott said, "What do you think happened to get Ruby's sister back in her life suddenly? If you thought that was just a normal and natural occurrence, let me clarify it was not so at all, it was all staged and well-rehearsed. Ruby's sister was brought in to ensure Ruby was safe and to get you out of this house for a weekend."

Scott told him the real plan to get him away from the house was to bug the house with camera and microphones and more importantly Scott wanted to spend some time with his son. The living room where we are sitting and almost every other room of this house had hidden camera for video recording and small microphones to record voice.

Neil in his mind started to replay all the different days since returning from that wonderful holiday to see if he could remember something, which he could use to pin it on Ruby, unfortunately nothing seemed to stand out. Moreover it also occurred to him since Ruby was aware of the surveillance in the house being active, she would not have said anything which could be used against her later.

21

Sam was truly devastated that he was beaten by Ruby not once but repeatedly. He did not know what he could say or do to get some leverage from this adverse situation he found himself in.

He looked at Scott and finally asked "So what now?" Scott looked at him and said-" What do you want it to be Neil? I want you to leave Ruby with all the material possessions you own, all your bank accounts and an unconditional divorce." Scott further added "You would also give the full custody of the children to Ruby."

Sam waited to hear if there was more to it, after a few seconds when nothing else was added, he looked at Ruby and said, " I hope what you have done makes you happy?" Ruby did not bother to reply but put up a great show of being the poor tormented soul going through a lot of pain.

Neil told Scott, "I agree with your terms but I have a condition, I will do as you want me to do and go away from your life and your world. I only want an assurance you will not hunt me down and rock my world." Scott looked at Neil and said, "You tread lightly and don't step on our toes and we will not on yours."

Scott called his lawyer, briefed him to make all agreements and arrange for them to be properly executed in the court. Neil told Scott he would sign the papers before the weekend and leave the town.

Sam asked to go to his room and get his passport and other travel documents, Scott waved him off but cautioned him not to try any tricks. Neil looked at Scott and said "There is nothing to try, what you see in front of you is a body with no soul." Sam without waiting for Scott's response climbed up the stairs.

He quickly took his passport and other things of immediate need in a small bag. He managed to slip in his personal laptop into it too. He then took out the small knife he kept in his bedside drawer and came down while hiding the knife in his left hand and holding the bag on his left shoulder. Once on the ground floor Sam took the bag from his shoulder put it on ground and extended the trolley.

Sam passed close to Scott and pretended to lose his bag's grip. While Scott tried to look at the bag, Sam quickly lashed at him, and managed to make a large cut on his left arm. Sam roared into a laughter and whispered to Scott "This is my last and final gift of pain to you."

Ruby started to scream when she saw blood oozing out of Scott's arm. Sam took his bag and quickly ran out of the door. He called a taxi on the run and was lucky to get one before he reached the main road. He told the driver to drive away. Sam got down at the next highway bus station, bought a ticket for the bus and boarded the bus.

Meanwhile back home Ruby ran out to her car and took Scott to the nearest clinic. The doctor wanted them to lodge a police complaint for assault but Scott declined. Ruby tried to argue with him but Scott was adamant that he did not want police to be involved. Doctor gave a local anesthesia, put six sutures on his arm and a dressing on it. He told them to come again in two days to get the dressing replaced. He also gave him a prescription for painkillers.

On the way home Scott told Ruby that it was a small retaliation of a person who had lost everything. He further added, Don't worry he will be coming back on friday to sign the papers and I will ensure he pays for this. Scott took out his phone and called a friend who worked as a bouncer in a local club and arranged for him to have few of his friends with him on friday to give a small farewell to Neil after he has signed the papers.

Ruby parked the car in the driveway and asked Scott, if he would stay for the night in the guest room or would he like to go home. Scott told her he would like to go home but before he leaves he needs to make a phone call and ensure Ruby and kids would be safe in the house.

Scott told Ruby , I am sure Neil is not crazy enough to come back again, especially knowing the house is full of cameras and microphones. If he does I am going to make sure the local police is aware of the danger he poses and he would be arrested if he comes within the boundary of this house. Scott called a buddy from the local police department and explained to him the situation. Scott told him to arrange some surveillance of the area for one night at least.

Scott left for his home in a taxi leaving his own car behind. Once he was home his parents were not pleased to see his arm in a bandage again. Scott had a shower and ate dinner at his parents place. Later Scott once alone called up Ruby and asked her if everything was ok and if the kids were in bed? Once Ruby confirmed everything was ok, Scott called up his lawyers to ensure all paperwork was being progressed for Neil to sign as discussed.

Next few days were quite uneventful, and then came Friday. Ruby and Scott came over to their lawyer's office a little before time to check and verify that all papers were correctly drafted. Scott asked the lawyer for the papers, he scanned quickly and found them in order he passed the papers to Ruby for her to check. Meanwhile he went out to call his friend to ensure the welcome party would be ready to deal with Neil once the papers were signed and he was leaving the lawyer's office.

At exactly 1100 hours Neil's lawyer came in and asked the papers to be presented. When Scott asked about whereabouts of Neil the lawyer said, if you deliver the papers I will get them duly signed. I have power of attorney from my client to represent him today and to complete the legal documents. I have a message from my client for you too. Let me first complete these legal formalities then we can close out the personal matters.

He checked all the documents, put it in a docket and called his assistant to take the papers from him for signatures, and once the papers were handed over to the assistant, he turned to Scott and Ruby and said, "Can we talk somewhere in private." Scott nodded and invited him to the other room. Once they were in the room, Neil's lawyer made a show of closing the door and then told Scott, My client Mr.Neil is afraid of you and your friends trying to inflict pain to him He reminds you that you had given your word to not follow him or hunt him down anymore once the papers are signed."

"And if you are wondering how he knew please see the phone you used, unfortunately it is the same phone he gave you..!!" Scott realized his mistake and told the lawyer to tell him where Neil was or else he would suffer. The lawyer looked at him and laughed, "To be honest, I am not even aware where he has gone after signing the papers, my fees was paid by him in advance and I was compensated for a few broken bones too, however I do hope you would not go through the trouble to give me that unnecessary trouble. I can assure you I have no forwarding address of Mr.Neil and while we were in this room he would have already left for where ever he is going."

Scott ran out, saw the papers lying on his lawyer's table, with no trace of the lawyer's assistant. On top of the papers was a small sticker with a smiley and a message "Lets be strangers" Scott called up his friend and told him to spread out and look for Neil. Then he smashed his handset on the floor. Ruby came out at the sound of the phone being smashed and also saw the note... She felt Neil was more like her who did not leave any game without him winning it. She was pretty sure Neil had a stash hidden somewhere which she had no clue about and he would be currently heading to where ever that was kept.

Ruby looked at Scott and both knew Neil had given them the slip. The last parting stroke Scott had planned would not be happening anymore. Ruby was only happy that she would have Scott to give her all she dreamt of for many years to come. Ruby thought she played her cards well.

Scott would take a while to come around and get over the disappointment of having missed out on his finale but Ruby knew he would not hold it against her and unless she did something really stupid, Scott would stay with her and her children would have a comfortable life and a doting father.

Neil had a few busy days since he had last run in with Scott. He had been in touch with his prison mates family and relatives. He had been collecting the money from a few of them as per his projection to make a fast profit for them. The collection was not a small change by any standard and he had almost all of it in cash with him, some cheques which he had encashed into his personal account. He had used this to pay off his debts, and clear his other obligations. The balance cash he had withdrawn from his account.

He had no intention of leaving any trace whereby the money would tie to him, From now on he was going to be a nobody in this country. He was waiting to retrieve his new identity papers to be delivered so that he could leave the country and start a new life.

Neil knew Scott would send his people looking for him. Neil after he had signed the papers in the lawyers assistant car strolled down to the metro and took a train. Sam was sure people would be looking for him in and around the lawyer's office but no one would think of covering the local transport. Even if they did, it would not be easy with lot of tourists and commuters boarding the trains at every station.

Sam had also changed his appearance drastically in last few days. He shaved off his head and grew a beard. This morning when he got up to get ready, he himself had a shock when he looked in the mirror. Neil knew he looked quite different from his pictures and though he has been in news recently, he in his current avatar did not look anything like his own self. He was also dressed quite casually in a blue jeans and T shirt which was quite different from all his public appearances which previously were all in a suit, with a well groomed mane and clean shaven face.

Sam travelled to the central station and took the first train out of the city. He was traveling with only a suitcase and a backpack like any other tourist. He was thankful he had invested in his second identity a few months back. He was headed in the right direction with nobody in the know where he was headed.

Neil had no phone with him or any other electronic device which could be used to trace him. Sam had dumped all his electronic devices last night in a dumpster and had no intention to be socially or professionally active on the internet anytime soon, if possible never.

Sam was going to fly below the radar detection range, go to a different continent and stay away from big towns. Sam believed he had enough money in cash to not require any bank accounts for a while and just relax. Sam was not bothered what would happen once his "friends" were released from prison, they would surely come looking for him and he would not exist. He had been careful to ensure no one knew his future plan. Even people who had helped him only knew bits and pieces. Sam did not trust anyone to divulge all the details of his plan.

Sam had told everyone his address and house he shared with Ruby and they would go looking there. Sam thought of it and smiled - When Ruby was confronted by these rough guys, how she will handle it. Sam knew initially she will try to dissociate herself from Neil. Sam also knew his friends would not forget about the money, they would not care who gave it back as far as they got their money back. Neil hoped Ruby or at least Scott would see reason in it and pay even a million dollars if they had to give to buy peace. Sam thought that was justice served to Ruby for double crossing him and humiliating him all this time. He told himself I am a very reasonable man, I am only taking the fifty percent of what she should have given me of that two million dollars years back.

How Sam wished he could stay back and watch that episode unfold but he knew staying in this continent was dangerous for him. Sam has realized the flashes in his dreams do come true at worst of the times. Although he could not see them clearly he knew not to tempt fate. If he followed his instinct and avoided being in situations in his dreams he would live longer and possibly happier

Sam tried to sketch the place he usually saw himself in, the details were a bit unclear but it seemed a nice tropical island with lots of sun and he attired in T-shirt and shorts. Sam started to plan where he would go next. He knew if he gave it a thought, his own subconscious mind would take him to the right place.

Sam knew the place must not be not a popular tourist destination and /or possibly a place where he can rest, survive for a few years while the heat dissipated and people stopped looking for him. Neil wanted to go to a small suburban town with few people so he can set up a small business and make an "honest" and quiet living. Coming from a person who has relied on unfair practices to collect his wealth, this seemed quite ironic.

Sam waited for almost a week to ensure no one was looking for him. He kept moving every few days all the time moving away from town where he had left Ruby and others. Sam was close to moving out of his native country and knowing how it can be a trouble to carry so much cash with him. Sam knew if he went to an airport and his suitcase was checked he would have no reasonable explanation for why he was carrying so much cash.

Considering the current political and religious sentiments he was sure he would either be arrested for being a terrorist or else without a legal explanation his wealth would have to be confiscated till he could submit some official explanation for it. He had travelled by road so far and his plan was to book a luxury liner berth and sail away. He really had no fixed routine or pressing agenda which he had to follow except to remain invisible.

Sam was waiting for that single place that would look remotely similar to the place of his dream or his destiny to guide him. Neil was not staying at rundown hotels due to his fear that such places would be frequented by people who would be looking for an opportunity to swindle others. Sam also knew and believed such places were always on the radar of local police and goons alike, and he was trying to avoid any trouble.

Sam was not staying at luxury hotel either as he suspected his friends from the past or Scott would be expecting him to stay in style with the money he had. He was living a life of a normal random man, a person who would just disappear and melt away in other millions of people around him and stay unidentified.

Sam had no ambition of glory anymore and he was happy being one of the zillion people as far as he could have a comfortable life. He had enough money and all he had to do was to stay sensible.

If Neil was sensible he would live a lot longer...But then Sam could never be quiet....

22

Neil is sleeping well but had a strange dream last night. It took him back to his childhood..

Neil is 8 years old. He is right in the middle of a battle with his friend Rahim with his sword. He has drawn first blood but Rahim does not agree with him and this is making him angry.

Neil is the third child in a family of five kids. He has an elder brother, and sister who always seem to be telling him what to do and what not to do. He is only 8 but already had his fill with his elder siblings telling him what he can do or not. His two younger sisters are afraid of him and live in his awe. Neil is the smartest one in his family. Neil's elder brother is always struggling to get acceptable grades and usually barely manages to get through to the next grade. His sisters are good in music, dance and other extra-curricular activities but none of them is like Neil.

Neil has near photographic memory and needs to only listen or read it once to be able to reproduce it again without much effort. He is normally at the top of his class if not then he is a close second or third. This had made Neil feel as if the world owes him some gratitude to be living with the other earthly beings.

All the teachers at school have only good things to say about Neil and this is very quickly going to his head. He dreams of being a king, but wait, we do not have kings any more but then for an 8 year old reality and dreams are one and the same. He thinks everything is within his grasp and he has to only say it only once and things will come to him.

Today is different his friend does not agree with him and his anger is rising. His friend thinks he has lost the battle but he has clearly won it. His friend Rahim is teasing him as Neil has done so many times in the past and never thought of how anyone else feels. Neil the invincible has been defeated. He is a few steps behind Rahim now who has a spring in his feet and is in a hurry to go home to narrate to anyone who would hear how he had defeated Neil.

Neil cannot seem to be able to stop Rahim from blabbering, Rahim is looking back at him and walking, Neil can see a snag and a bit of uneven ground in front of his friends feet and suddenly Sam is telling him, "Let Rahim trip and fall. He should break his leg and cry in pain. He should have so much of pain that he forgets his victory march and be at my mercy to be rescued."

What happens next is a shock for Neil- in a split second his friend has fallen and is crying in pain. He is unable to move his left foot and right arm at all. There is also some blood on his face and forearm. Neil runs upto Rahim tries to help him sit up and give him some water but his friend is not able to drink and is howling. It is getting dark and they have to hurry home. His bravery seems to be disappearing and all the ghostly images, which he and Rahim have discussed about from his comic books, flash in front of his eyes. His friend is afraid and crying. Rahim says, "Neil, the ghosts will come and eat me Please will you save me?

Neil has to do something, he tells his friend to not worry and that he would stand guard for him. But then his friend moves a little and cries out loud in pain. Neil does not know what he can do. They are not very far from the compound but there are no street lights. This happens quite frequently when they have Army exercises in the defense station, the area is literally so dark you can not see a few metres in front of you.

Neil tells his friend he is going to get help and starts to run leaving his friend with complete stock of his weapons- 2 swords 3 guns and his armour for extra precaution. All he has with him is the little knife he carries with him all the time. He runs towards home, the watchman at the gate of the compound asks him where Rahim is but he does not stop and keeps running to find his own house door closed. He does not know where is every one then he remembers it is world cup final day and everyone would be at Doctor Singh's house, who had the only working color TV in the whole neighbourhood

He runs quickly towards Doctor Singh's house. He can hear some loud sounds from inside. He makes a dramatic entry in the room with his hair all dishevelled, sweat dripping, and clothes full of dirt. He does not even bother to take off his shoes and walks all over the carpet with his muddy shoes. He shouts "Rahim is in pain, with blood oozing out and he is not able to move his arms and legs. He is lying near the football field outside the compound, with no lights." He proudly declares although still breathless – "Don't worry, I left him with my armour, swords and guns to keep him safe.

Doctor Singh rushes out with his assistant and a stretcher to find Rahim and bring him back to hospital for treatment. The ambulance with a stretcher in it and a wailing siren leaves the compound. Neil's mom and others start fussing over him. Neil's mom is complaining that she does not understand how he gets so dirty every day. His dad is arguing with his mom telling her to let kids be kids and let them enjoy life. Neil starts praying to God "please let this not be a screaming and arguing match between them." Thankfully it does not boil over and just fizzles out after a few murmurs exchanged between them to not make a scene in the public.

The attention is back on Neil now. He can feel the pride in mom's voice how her son is brave and saved his friend. While Neil is having a battle with Sam within, "Why did he wish for Rahim to be hurt?" Neil does get this conflict all the time. Another incident comes to his mind when Sam told him to punish one of his friends for not listening to him and Neil kicked up muddy water on his clothes and later feigned innocence. Neil is wondering if he had pushed Rahim? Or was it Sam?

Neil does not know why but sometimes he feels Sam is the evil person in the stories that mom and dad read to him where the evil guy is responsible for all the bad things which happen. This tussle within him causes more internal conflict and there is no way to deal with it. Neil not knowing what to do starts to cry aloud. No one seems to understand what happened to him.

People start to look at Neil and now Neil is back in the spotlight with people around him fussing over him, getting him water and pacifying him with sweets.

Rahim is brought in a stretcher, his arms and legs are all bandaged and he is still in some pain. Neil hears the Doctor tell his parents "It will be few weeks before he recovers as he has two fractures." A part of Neil is happy that this year in final exams he would have one competitor less.

A few days pass by and Neil's mom tells Neil to go and play with Rahim. But Neil doesn't want to go as Rahim is lying in bed with his arm and leg held in a cast. Rahim cannot play or run with others. Neil's mom lectures him on how important it is to take care of friends as these friends from early life remain your true friends later in life. With no other kids in his age group in the Cantonment Neil does not have any choice.

Neil goes to Rahim's place and sits with him for a while. Rahim's mom says how nice it is of Neil to come and Rahim is happy to chat with him. Rahim has so many questions about school and who is doing what prank in the class. Neil is supposed to be helping Rahim with his classwork and studies while Rahim is in bed recovering.

Rahim recovers fully and comes back to school, although he does not challenge Neil in studies this year and Neil stands first and enjoys the attention he gets.

One thing Neil has never really been clear about was there really a snag or was it Neil or Sam who had pushed Rahim and made it look like an accident.

After all these years, Neil still faces this conflict. Sam laughs at Neil when Neil asks him this question. Sam always says, "This question is for you to answer", Do you Neil, feel guilty for pushing your friend to fall and get hurt?, or do want to blame someone else who does not even exist..

OOO

Excerpts from "Ruby - the random woman"

She was woken up by the buzz of her phone- she looked it was a Good morning beautiful from Jim. She smiled; he was trying hard to impress her. She thought of replying to him, but then old Ruby took over and told her Nahh, you don't reply.!! So, she tossed the phone on the bed and went to get ready for college. She got another text around noon asking her to meet Jim for dinner at 8 am, she looked at the message again, "Shall we meet for dinner at *8*"JIM, who writes his name in capitals!!??, She thought to herself and my God this guy is too formal he needs to ease up a bit!! She wrote up - Do you always invite everyone this way? RUBY

She thought she was being funny, but he replied - Good Day, I don't normally get a chance to invite, JIM, she again laughed at the message and did not reply this time. She got another message in 10 minutes, can you please confirm if 8 is ok for you? Jim, she replied I do not know unless you tell me where? Jim replied I will pick you up from your house, let us say I will be there at 7:30 pm, to keep the time of dinner for 8 pm- JIM. Once again Ruby laughed at all the grammar punctuations and writing his name after every message, she found it quite strange that he would be so British in his approach, or at least that is what they called guys you were well mannered and talked in Shakespeare English! At college.

For her and her friends if it is not in SMS abbreviated text then it is too literal!!

She wrote back - OK, C U ltr, she went home and slept for a while as she wanted to be fresh and perky at dinner. She got up at 5 pm, had a shower and then while rolling her hair started looking for a dress to wear, she changed 3 times but was not still fully satisfied then she saw her off-shoulder dress which she had bought last month and never worn, she quickly took it off and cut out its price tag and ironed it in a hurry and tried it on ..!! Yeah, it was perfect, sensual but not showy, she teamed it up with a nice pair of stilettos and then took the heels off to get her to make up done. She spend the next 45 minutes in front of the mirror and only realized it was time when the phone rang to announce the arrival of Jim at her door.

Ruby took her clutch from the bed, opened and dropped her phone into it, pushed the heels on, and moved out of her room. Aunt looked at her and gestured the slaughter with her left thumb and then lolled her head to one side with tongue hanging, Ruby smiled at her and bid her goodbye, Her aunt said I hope you are wearing something under that dress and whatever it is, keep it on its the first date..!! Ruby just shook her head and carried on.!!Ruby came outside to see a black shiny Rolls Royce at her door with Jim standing with an open door and looking really handsome in a black suit, Ruby suddenly thought she was underdressed but when she was the look of admiration on Jim's face all her apprehension just evaporated. He took her arm kissed her on each cheek and helped her inside the car then softly closed the door and hurriedly walked to the other side to enter the car told the driver, let's go...

Ruby was still trying to guess about where they were going, so she said I hope I am not being kidnapped, Jim smiled and said Not today!! I hope you like Italian food; this place is awesome and one of my favorites to enjoy Italian food. Ruby said - For me food is secondary, it is the atmosphere and the company which makes it awesome...She tilted her head and looked at Jim's face while smiling a bit, she could see Jim's eyes like a puppy who wanted to be petted. Ruby knew she was leading Jim on, but she also knew she was in control for now. She asked Jim, how was your day? Jim replied, A bit busy but nothing out of ordinary. And further asked her, Are you from around here? Ruby said No, I am not, I came to live with my aunt so that I can pursue my dream to be an actress. Jim smiled and said- For a beautiful girl like you it should not be difficult, I have a lot of contacts and can help you. Ruby looked at him leaned in a bit and said seductively but why would you?? And smiled again. Before Jim could reply, the driver announced they had arrived at the destination.

Jim sprang out of his seat even before the car was stationary and opened the door for Ruby and offered her his arm. Like a true gentleman and they went to the Italian restaurant, there seemed like a sort of queue waiting to get in but Jim was directly ushered in and shown to a table in a corner which was a bit secluded from others but still had a view of inside and outside. The manager who accompanied them asked if they would like the usual wine, looking at Jim who asked Ruby if wine would be okay for her. Ruby nodded and said thank you.

****

Ruby had a rush of emotions that finally she had won something, and her career path may take off now. She did not answer him and walked off for the photo session with the other winners. One of the Judges had to put the winner sash on Ruby and while doing so he touched and rubbed her back. His touch made her skin crawl and she cringed inwardly. She inhaled sharply but kept the smile to not let this spoil her happiness. While the photographs were being taken the judges tried to grope and touch Ruby and other girls. She finally managed to get away from their grasp as soon as photographs were done.

Ruby came home with her aunt and on the way was telling her aunt about the behavior of these leeches at the event. Her aunt patted her hand and told her I am sure this is not the first time, and neither is this the last time you would experience this. Her aunt told her to be ready to be scrutinized every day by many men some of them who could be even your father. If we all can only get through with our lives with only ogling and some occasional touches the world would be still a happy place. Her aunt further added I am not trying to justify their behavior it makes my skin crawl even hearing of such behavior or even the thought of it but the fact is, it does happen. We as women need to aware of it, prepare for it, and retaliate if it goes beyond a limit. We need to define the limit and listening to what you just told me this is the limit, any further and I am sure you would have hit him so hard that he would not look at a girl for a while.

Both shared a smile at that thought and then Ruby added but the young judge who is the son the famous builder although was flirting too but was not frisky, and this only got her aunt to start teasing her. Her aunt asked so do you plan to go out with him?, Ruby made a face, smiled, and said "Fat chance", I did not give him my number or ask him!, her Aunt pouted and said What a pity gal!. Both were enjoying this, it was like old times when they could sit and talk for hours. Once home Ruby asked her Aunt, when I get my new car we would have to park yours on the road outside as my new car would need to be in the garage!, Aunty smiled and said, This is my house and my garage so your car can be on the road, my car has so many sentimental memories. Ruby added Nahh it has only mental values, it drives anyone driving it nuts.!!

Both of them were exhausted from the longish day but were enjoying the light banter and then her aunt opened a bottle of wine and asked her to get 2 glasses, both of them kicked off their shoes and sat on the open deck listening to the sound of the sea crashing on the shore. They both walked off and sat on the wooden deck dangling their legs while sipping the wine. Both were lost in their world yet happy to have someone near them to share.Suddenly there was a rumble of thunder, followed by a bolt of lightning and it suddenly started to pour down heavily, Both of them picked their glasses, jumped with glee and ran towards the beach, enjoying the rain and dancing to the sound of water on the tin roof of a nearby shack.

After a while, her aunt said I cannot even feel my legs, and before I collapse here let me get indoors. Both, Ruby and her aunt ran back to the deck, Ruby's aunt sat on a chair and started breathing heavily, Ruby went inside and got her a set of fresh towels. Both of them removed their wet clothes and sat wrapped up in towels sipping their wine and looking at the lights of the big ships anchored far away in the bay. Finally, her Aunt spoke - Ruby you know what? Let us go inside, it is getting cold!! Both were a bit tipsy and found it funny that they were balancing the glasses and walking swaying. All this time giggling and laughing out loud, they tumbled in. Both just dropped on the bed in towels and soon were snoring under the effect of alcohol and being already tired from the long and quite an activity-filled day.

The next morning, Ruby finished her yogurt and kept sitting on the kitchen stool watching the waves breaking outside till she was a bit sleepy with the soothing sound of the ocean. She got up lazily and went back to her room and slipped under the covers again.

****